GENESIS *versus* DARWINISM:

ABRIDGED VERSION

ESPECIALLY FOR ADVENTISTS

GENESIS *versus* DARWINISM:

ABRIDGED VERSION

ESPECIALLY FOR ADVENTISTS

by Desmond Ford
PhD, MSU
PhD, Manchester

Genesis versus Darwinism:

ABRIDGED VERSION ESPECIALLY FOR ADVENTISTS

Desmond Ford

A copy of this book may be found in
the National Library of Australia

Religion / Christian Education / General
228 pages

Cover design by Gillian Ford
Image: Canstock; Photo: Gillian Ford
Typeface (text): Adobe Caslon Pro

This book may be ordered through www.amazon.com, bookseller, or online retailers.

Desmond Ford has written many books on the gospel of Christ. He is the founder of "Good News Unlimited," a nonprofit organization which publishes a newsletter, offers online video presentations and facilitates worship services (www.goodnewsunlimited.org).

Printed in the United States of America

DEDICATION

Gill made me do it, and without her
it would not have been made.

Testimony & Quotes

"I have used figures of speech to tell you these things ..." (John 16:25, *Good News Bible*).

In my teens in the 1940s, like most other Christians, I believed the earth to be about 6,000 years old. Twenty years later I fellowshipped with a very wonderful Christian, Dr. Eric Magnusson, who had two Ph.Ds. in science, and I learned my error. After another forty years I walked Florida beaches with Dr. and Mrs. Peter Hare and learned much more. It was also my privilege to be in the home of Dr. Richard Ritland and listen to him. These scientists (each of whom had once believed as I did as a teenager that the earth was about 6,000 years old) encouraged me to study much further on these issues. When challenged to a debate with a professor from the University of California, Sacramento, I spent over a hundred hours preparing for that event. Many of my views were then consolidated. They are represented in this book.
Desmond Ford

Well-read evangelical scholars know that Darwin has been proved wrong about the Malthusian struggle (the cornerstone for natural selection), gradualism, his theory of heredity (the gemmules), sexual selection (the main theme in *The Descent of Man)*, survival of the fittest, absolute uniformitarianism, the reasons for extinctions, etc. As Gould said decades ago, "Darwinism is 'effectively dead.'" See Norman Macbeth's *Darwin Retried* for a concise summary. Therefore, for evangelical scholars the tension between Genesis and Darwinism has been dissolved by the march of science.
Desmond Ford

Darwin helped "lay the foundation for the bloodiest war in history," declared the pacifist William Jennings Bryan. ... William Roscoe Thayer, in his presidential address to the American Historical Association in 1918 stated:

> I do not believe that the atrocious war into which the Germans plunged Europe in August, 1914, and which has subsequently involved all lands and all peoples, would ever have been fought, or at least would have attained its actual gigantic proportions, had the Germans not been made mad by the theory of the survival of the fittest.
> Quoted in Antonella La Vergata, "Evolution and War, 1871-1918," *Nuncio,* Vol. 9, 1994, page 148, in Richard Weikart, *From Darwin to Hitler: Evolutionary Ethics, Eugenics, and Racism in Germany,* New York, Palgrave-Macmillan, 2004, page 164

The universe and the laws of physics seem to have been specifically designed for us. If any one of about 40 physical qualities had more than slightly different values, life as we know it could not exist. Either atoms would not be stable, or they wouldn't combine into molecules, or the stars wouldn't form the heavier elements, or the universe would collapse before life could develop, and so on.
Stephen Hawking, *Austin American-Statesman,* October 19, 1997

Darwin himself, in a letter to the famous botanist Bentham, confesses that "The belief in natural selection must at present be grounded entirely on general causes: when we descend to details we can prove that no one species has changed: nor can we prove that the supposed changes are beneficial which is the groundwork of the theory"[1]—a most amazing statement from Darwin.

"It [*The Origin of Species*] is a mere rag of a hypothesis with as many flaws and holes as sound parts"
Darwin's words spoken to Thomas Huxley, quoted by Janet Browne, *Charles Darwin: The Power of Place,* page 53

---

1   Francis Darwin, *Life and Letters of Charles Darwin,* II, page 210, in Wilbur M. Smith, *Therefore Stand,* Boston, MA, 1945, p 326.

When we understand how the Fall in Eden and the Atonement of Calvary fit together like key and lock we shall never again doubt the historicity of Genesis 3 and its deep theological importance, despite its obvious symbolism.
Desmond Ford

Why do we protest so vigorously about things beyond our knowledge and for which we have no answer? Are there not a million mysteries in our immediate environment for which we have no solution? Christ says, "What is that to thee? Follow thou me."
Desmond Ford

Genesis is not anti-scientific nor pre-scientific, but non-scientific. Scientific views change from generation to generation, but holiness, the reflection of God, never changes. And there can be no lasting happiness without holiness. Sin is suicide and insanity, but purity is paradise. How very practical Scripture is! History can be interpreted in many different ways, and historians differ in their opinion, but holiness is so clearly identified in the person of Jesus Christ that all unanswered questions have little weight.
Desmond Ford

"I believe in Heaven, nothing else makes sense of Earth."

TABLE OF CONTENTS

ABRIDGED BOOK

Chapter	Title	Page No.

FOREWORD

This may be the most important book you have ever read. The title may sound abstract but the substance is actually about you. From morning to night we make decisions, and the important ones depend on what we think is true about our world—particularly its origin. If you decide that everything came about by chance it obviously is not going to matter much whether you decide one way or another. After all, you are only here a little while, the toy of chance and circumstance, and soon by accident or sickness your life will be over. And that's that.

On the other hand, if you believe that this world is not a chance product but one carefully designed for you and all others, your decision is going to be different. There could be a reckoning day after death, and maybe right now there is a Supreme Being with his eye on you, who loves you despite your weaknesses and follies. And so, that's what this book is about.

This book is an abridgement of a very much larger volume, one filled with quotations from scientists and philosophers. But I have been asked to write a small book without too many learned quotes. If you want those which substantiate the views here offered read the larger book. There will be some key quotes here, but only a few compared to the large version.

Here are some basic facts that every intelligent person must take into account. Scientists affirm that the universe is nearly 14 billion years old and this planet about 4-and-a-half billion. The history of our world is found in what is known as the Geologic Column—earth's strata, layered one on top of another, with the most recent last. The succession is the same all over the world though earthquakes and other upheavals can at times change part of the sequence. These strata contain fossils most of which are from creatures no longer living in our world.

As we near the top of the column we find fossils of creatures with which we are familiar, but no humans until we are almost at the top. Radiometric dating (based on radioactive decay of elements like uranium) reveals the age of each strata and therefore also the age of the creatures whose skeletal remains are embedded in these strata. Radiocarbon dating can only extend accurately to 50,000 years, so for the rocks geologists choose radiometric dating.

There are over fifty different methods of calculating the age of this earth. And they agree. Only the ignorant dispute this. But if you ever went to Sunday School you may have some questions. If you are like me, you were taught that the earth is about 6,000 years old as is inscribed in the margin of some King James Version Bibles. Furthermore, if you knew anything about the Geologic Column, you might have been told that its contents belong to one generation, that of Noah's Flood.

In addition there are some rather strange things you may remember from Sunday School—like the early men who lived to nearly one thousand years, and the giants of Noah's day, and the Tower of Babel which aimed at heaven. It's all rather puzzling. Maybe you are a confirmed Christian, and the more you learn about scientific conclusions the more bewildered you are with these 'strange anomalies' in the Bible.

If you are still in your twenties or younger and you go to university, you will find any trust you have in the Bible assaulted there. The likelihood is very considerable that you will decide to grow up and abandon your "childish" beliefs.

But what most of your university teachers will not tell you is that there are many very gifted and highly educated people who still trust in the Bible and who do not believe that the Geologic Column is the result of either Noah's Flood or Darwin's theory of evolution. Almost certainly you will not be informed that now there are thousands of scientists who are not Christians who also reject much that was taught by Charles Darwin.

If you want to test this out quickly, buy (or procure a copy through inter-library loan), *Evolution: a Theory in Crisis* by molecular scientist Michael Denton. The book has been challenged on the basis of philosophical vagaries, but not successfully countered with scientific objections. Get it and see. It is the best book on the topic. The next best is *Creation or Evolution* by physicist Alan Hayward.

Should you run into one of these many Christian scholars who object to the popular teachings about evolution they may also refer you to books like *Old Testament Survey* by Lasor, Hubbard, and Bush. This book explains what most scholarly Christians know, that Genesis chapters 1-11 is full of allusions to ancient realities, but they are presented in parabolic form under divine inspiration for excellent reasons.

But perhaps you are not sure the Bible should be bothered with. Let me offer you a few facts about that. The Bible is the most unique book in the world—a library with many types of literature ranging over about fifteen centuries. It has been the inspiration of countless multitudes of people who have made our world a better place. Its central figure is Jesus of Nazareth, who on the last Tuesday of his life, declared, "Heaven and earth, will pass away, but my words will never pass away" (Matt. 24:35). Out of the approximately ten billion people who have lived on this planet Christ is the only one who has made such a remarkable claim. And twenty centuries have confirmed the likelihood of its complete fulfillment.

When a loving follower anointed his feet a few days before his crucifixion Christ predicted that her act would be known throughout all coming days and rehearsed wherever his gospel was preached. See John's Gospel chapter 12. He also foretold that the time would come when his gospel would go to the whole world in the last generation. See Matthew 24:14 and Acts 1:8. Remember there were no printing presses then, and no TV, no computers or Internet. Again Jesus claimed to be "the Light of the World" (see John 8:12). It is a certain fact of history that no other person has ever shed so much light on the meaning of life and the way to immortality.

This same Galilean, after three days in the tomb, appeared to his disillusioned followers. Five hundred saw him all at once, and he tarried among them for forty days. See 1 Corinthians 15 and Acts chapter 1.

Now, you can explain a puddle in the road by talking about a summer shower, but you cannot explain the Gulf Stream that way. What on earth could have transformed brokenhearted people and turned so many into missionaries and martyrs?

Of course it had all been predicted centuries ago. Read Isaiah 52:12 to the end of chapter 53, which tells of the coming Messiah whose life would be "cut off" and yet who would "prolong his days." It had been typified by the rising of Isaac from the altar on Mount Moriah two thousand years earlier, and by Jonah's deliverance from the whale's belly after three days.

If you doubt the Bible just read Genesis 12:1-3 which predicts that a wandering Bedouin in the ancient near east would one day be reverenced by all the nations of the world. And so it has happened. Muslims, Jews, and Christians in every land look to Abraham as their spiritual father. What are the chances of that prophecy being fulfilled?—about one in billions.

Do not neglect the prophecies. I have written commentaries on *Daniel and Revelation* that you may one day read. In the meantime just read Daniel 9:24-27, which forecasts the coming of Christ within approximately five centuries from the rebuilding of the ruined Jewish temple. More than that—this passage also says he would be put to death and that one of the results would be the desolation of the famous temple worshipped by those responsible for his death. And don't fail to note that it is also said that those who rejected him would experience desolation until the end of time.

There are hundreds of other prophecies, but what I have referred to can make a good start. If God made the world, would you not expect that he would tell us about it and confirm his words by things out of the ordinary? That is exactly what has happened.

Have you heard of the Anthropic Principle? About forty years ago a scientist from Oxford told a famous gathering of scientists that the evidence is now overwhelming that every law of physics was the result of minute crafting for the purpose of making our universe and us. There are lots of books and articles on that topic and it proves the reality of God. Had certain physical laws been different by a millionth of a millionth, neither you, nor the universe, would be here. Professor Antony Flew, the most famous atheist of the twentieth century, was converted a few years ago by studying this principle and thousands have followed in his wake.

That's a start. Now I intend to dig deeper and challenge you to think in the same direction. If you have a college degree you didn't get it by going to the movies or by sleeping. You had to think and meditate a lot. What you are now engaged upon is a thousand times more important than your college degree and it will take similar application. But it is worth the effort. It could mean eternal life and joy for you and your family. What follows, remember, is only an abridgement of a much larger work that I hope you will one day read.

[This Abridged Version also contains at the end seven articles that are written particularly for Seventh-day Adventists. Adventists have been involved since their early days in the debate over creationism versus evolution and the question of the Age of the Earth. The subject is implied in their name "Seventh-day Adventist," which focusses on the seventh-day Sabbath instituted in creation week and their belief in an imminent Second Coming of Christ. Their founder, Ellen G. White, believed in a 6,000-year creation and later acolytes, such as George McCready Price, have played a key role in fostering interest in the subject in fundamentalist Christian churches in America. Hence it seems appropriate to address some questions specific to Adventism.]

CHAPTER 1

God speaks, who will listen?

NEXT TO ITS failure to reflect the winsomeness of Christ, the church's biggest problem is that most educated people in the West reject the Bible because of its "unbelievable" account of Adam and Eve and the origin of the world. But are these doubts well founded? Or is there abundant evidence to support traditional confidence in the Christian faith?

This book is a defense of the Bible with special attention to Genesis and its opening chapters. I write with an eye not only on my contemporaries, but also on the coming generations. Mixing with families, I often contemplate the world their children will face on attaining maturity. This book will probably be read by some of them. One scholar (from Wheaton) who has considered this problem is John H. Walton. Here are his words from *The Lost World of Genesis One*, page 96:

> One of the sad statistics of the last 150 years is that increasing numbers of young people who were raised in the environment of a biblical faith began to pursue education and careers in the sciences and found themselves conflicted as they tried to sort out the claims of science and the claims of the faith they had been taught.

I am retired from teaching and have taught many hundreds of young people in college and seminary. As mentioned in the Foreword and now repeated for emphasis, I have found that often when students begin university work they have a variety of beliefs, which are traditions rather than truth, and it is painful for them to be challenged on these things. *Only five percent of adolescents raised in American evangelical homes have retained their faith.*[1] The situation is the same in Australia. The majority of them, after a little time in university, surrender their Christian commitment. To lessen this abandonment, this terrible hemorrhage, is one of the purposes of this book.

Aristotle said that all humans seek to know. But humans want more. We want to know that life is worth living. We would like to be assured that at the centre of the universe there is a warm heart, a powerful hand, and a providence that rules and overrules. Nature gives some hints: the testimony of our senses, blue sky, green grass, wonderful sunrises and sunsets, flavours and melodies, pets, friends, and love. But what shall we say of the book that claims over 2,000 times that the God of heaven is behind it?

It is a unique book that promises to show us the way, the truth, and the life. It is really a library that revolves, all of it, around the issues that confront us every day—pain, sorrow, sin, uncertainty, revenge, contentment, satisfaction, love, meaning, hope, and faith. There are nuggets of gold easily accessible in this biblical library of books. Handled without prejudice they can give us the assurance we seek. But can we trust the Bible and rely on it in times of nightmare and storm? See the supernatural predictions of Genesis 12:2,3; Deuteronomy 18:15-18; Matthew 24:35; Isaiah 52:12–53:12; Daniel 9:24-27; and Micah 5:2. These passages are not of human origin. Humans could not make the predictions here found. History has fulfilled and justified them. *And the great theme of this library is the love, mercy, forgiveness, and grace of God. That is beyond price.*

The foundation of this library is Genesis, and Genesis confronts the first time reader with real difficulties, especially if he is a typical modern. We hear much about seeming threats to Genesis—neo-Darwinism, fossils, punctuated equilibrium, rocks that are a

---

1   Many question this number, but none can question the recent reports from the largest evangelical body in USA—the Southern Baptist Church. In the Annual Church Profile, sixty percent of the more than 46,000 churches in the Southern Baptist Convention (SBC) reported no youth baptisms (ages 12 to 17) in 2012, and 80 percent reported only one or two baptisms among young adults (ages 18-29). See Internet article: "Southern Baptists Millennial Problem," www.thegospelcoalition.org/blogs/.../southern-baptists-millennial-problem/, accessed 30 Aug 2014. The same pessimistic report has been given for the last seven years.

myriad years old, and theistic evolution—and the man is not living who is familiar with all the arguments that lie behind these theories. But as Thomas Kuhn (*The Structure of Scientific Revolutions*) pointed out some years ago, we do know that many false scientific theories have been entertained long after their exponents feared they were false. A flat earth, the impossibility of continental drift, phlogiston, ether, steady state and oscillation theories of the universe, and geo-synclinal geological theory were all cherished after the evidence was in that they were wrong. Some of these erroneous beliefs were widely taught in schools and universities in my childhood. In view of these facts the fears of Christians when confronted with threatening scientific theories may be unnecessary and misplaced. Some of these contemporary ideas will die in coming years.

For millennia, men of science taught that life came about by chance. The best scientists do not believe that any more. While most scientists reject spontaneous generation of life—reflecting perhaps on the famous statistics of Hoyle and Wickramasinghe—there are some who still hope for the miraculous working of chance. When we remember how many pieces of information are necessary for the formation of an amoeba this hope seems farfetched. Francis Crick says that life must have come from extra-terrestrials! (F. Crick & L. E. Orgel, "Directed Panspermia," *Icarus*, Vol. 19, pages 341–346). *So those who reject God cannot even get to first base.*

There is a growing awareness that reality transcends our present confident assertions. We have learned more about the universe in the last fifty years or so than in all preceding centuries. And the new knowledge frequently eradicates the old. Science students often find that their third year changes much of what they learned in their first year. Even where truth is being grappled with, it can be rudimentary. Until 1953 our knowledge of the structure and function of the DNA molecule was very inadequate. Only recently has it become clear that most of the so-called junk DNA is actually indispensable. The ENCODE project recorded in *Nature* has proved that.

Stephen C. Meyer, in a chapter on modern science, has this to say:

During the twentieth century a quiet but remarkable shift has

occurred in science. Evidence from cosmology, physics and biology now tells a very different story than did the science of the late nineteenth century. Evidence from cosmology supports a finite universe, not an infinite one, while evidence from physics and biology has reopened the question of design.
Science and Christianity: Four Views, pages 140-141

Einstein confessed to his folly in holding for too long to aspects of popular science ultimately to be rejected. For example, he experienced great difficulty in accepting the evidence for the beginning of the universe—the Big Bang—though nowadays that is taken for granted by most physicists. (Remember it took centuries before the truth of Genesis 1:1 that the world had a beginning was acknowledged by the educated world.)

Are you looking for a book that can answer correctly all your questions? There is no such book, though printed volumes are like people, vastly different in the extent of their knowledge. It was perhaps Sir Isaac Newton who wrote the most influential of all scientific testaments. He confessed to being like a child taking out a mere spoonful from the vast ocean of truth.

The New Testament affirms that it is by faith that we understand the creation of the world. See Hebrews 11:1. But faith is not credulity; it is not fanaticism. True faith has an abundance of truth to support it. Nevertheless, if we take the inspired words seriously, it is obvious we will never be able to write in gold all the answers to questions concerning creation. When you and I, even if standing on a mountaintop, take in the unending view, all we have is a dot compared with what we cannot see. Recently we have learned that dark matter and dark energy occupies ninety-six percent of the universe. Only four percent is open to our view regardless of our magnificent telescopes and spacecrafts. The same is true about our mental views.

But let us suppose that we *did* know *everything* about the beginning of our world. Would we not be tempted to make God dispensable? We do know that if he came down over our town or city every night and recited the Ten Commandments true religion would die. Our obedience would be the fruit of fear, not faith.

The volume you are reading will offer abundant evidence that Genesis is supernaturally inspired. It will suggest the reasons for contemporary unbelief, and at least some of these will here be rebutted. It will endeavour to show that the everlasting gospel, the glorious good news of the forgiving grace of God, is plainly set forth even in the Bible's first book. It will also give the reasons why some traditions long cherished among us cannot stand.

CHAPTER ONE SUMMARY:

Most Christian youth who attend University give up their faith. This is because they have been taught at home and in church certain traditions that are erroneous—including a six-thousand-year-old earth. The Bible nowhere teaches that, and over fifty scientific methods prove that the earth is very, very, old.

University teachers usually scoff at Genesis chapters 1–3; they know little or nothing about how the Bible often uses metaphoric symbols or parabolic language, as in the Book of Revelation and in Christ's stories.

The evidence for the divine inspiration of all Scripture is overwhelming. Consider, for example, the prophecies of Genesis 12:2,3; Deuteronomy 18:15-19; Isaiah 52:12-53:12; Daniel 9:24-27; Micah 5:2; Malachi 1:11; Matthew 24:35 and John 12:32.

We have learned more about the universe in the last fifty years than in all preceding millennia. The Anthropic Principle, only formulated in the 1970s, proves that the universe is very precisely designed for our sakes. If one of the physical parameters were different by just one part in a trillion there would be no universe. There are at least about forty such instances of miraculous design. No longer do we have to believe such myths as: "everything came from nothing"; "from chaos came fine-tuning"; "from randomness came information", "from chaos came the eye, the ear, the brain, and a thousand other infinitely precise mechanisms made for man."

Most people believe what their preferences choose, not what the facts affirm. The reason for faith in long-refuted Darwinism is that people are afraid to accept God in case he makes demands of them. They do not know that God is infinitely loving and counts the very hairs of our heads.

CHAPTER TWO

The Most Important
Sentence Ever Written

Genesis 1:1.

"In the beginning God created the heavens and the earth."

IF YOU HAD a life as long as Methuselah's and were offered a fortune to come up with the best introduction possible for a book to be read by millions, could you do better than the author of the Bible's first book? Let us multiply Methuselah's age by one hundred. Would that help?

More people have read this opening sentence of Scripture than any other sentence ever written. Apollo commander Edgar Mitchell placed it on the moon in microfilm in sixteen different languages. But on this planet it is available to seven billion people, and often without the cost of a single cent.

A child can understand it, but a genius cannot plumb it. Confronted by a sometimes threatening world we are all children and need the assurance here given at the beginning of the Bible. This is our Father's world.

Dr G. L. Schroeder tells us that *evolution, dinosaurs, cavemen are all trivial circumstances when compared to the concept of a beginning.* For millennia, men believed the universe was eternal. Aristotle had so taught and he was still the "Bible" for many. Most scientists thought this in the days before the Big Bang became fashionable. The former editor-in-chief of the premier science journal *Nature* said the idea of a beginning for the universe was "philosophically unacceptable."

Einstein thought the same, but years later said his unbelief was his biggest blunder. This new discovery destroyed the cyclical view of time, which teaches that all events keep recurring and that there never could be an end. This was the belief of the pagan empires that had come and gone, and the belief of most humans. We will consider more about that later.

Another new idea was that energy and matter were interchangeable, but at least Einstein had informed the world about that. The Hebrew word here used for "created" in Genesis 1:1 is a term that is used only of God as the subject. The revelation of the true nature of the Creator had begun. He was omnipotent and cared about his children. Monotheism is the most important of all facts. It has made science possible and given assurance and peace to the open minded. It challenged the polytheism and idolatry which were ubiquitous throughout the ancient world. That one idea has changed the world infinitely for the better.

These words (Gen. 1:1) are a safeguard from dangerous and destructive errors. Atheism, polytheism, pantheism, dualism, agnosticism, materialism, eternity of matter, reign of chance, humanism, and astrology are all hereby condemned. In other words, *most of the sorrows of the ages springing from erroneous beliefs could have been prevented if people had taken to heart this sentence.* Would Napoleon have been responsible for the deaths of millions had he understood the depth of Genesis 1:1? He was an idolater. Napoleon was Napoleon's god. The same is true of Kaiser Wilhelm, Adolf Hitler, Idi Amin, Muammar Gaddafi, and countless others who have shed rivers of blood because of their greed and egotism.

Think of the pain and heartbreak that violation of the laws of the Decalogue has brought to millions. All that could have been prevented had this single verse been given its true worth. The Creator is necessarily our Judge, and we should so live as to meet him in peace. Sin is insanity and purity is paradise. The greatest of all tragedies is not being a saint. Genesis chapter 1 tells us that God is a caring Father, and that there is no need to be afraid of anything in his world.

This verse wipes out the cyclical view of time held for millennia by pagan societies and taught so vigorously by Nietzsche. The doctrine of eternal recurrence makes people valueless. If nothing can be lastingly changed, why try? For untold millions in pagan lands, this view of time has brought despair and hopelessness. But to understand Genesis 1:1 irradiates creation and all of time. Its fruits ultimately are faith, hope, and love.

If Genesis 1:1 is not true then there are no grounds for passion, and no reason that anything should be pursued or avoided. We must never forget that *if there is no God there is also no man—only flotsam and jetsam*. If there is no God, there is no man, no reason, no meaning, no right and wrong, no hope, no forgiveness, and no eternal life. Never did a single sentence comprehend so much, and never did a single sentence have such infinite worth.

This first chapter of the Bible so wonderfully introduced offers both a history and a prophecy, and it is not by chance that this verse and the book it introduces is available anywhere on the planet and is in your hands today. God so loves us that he has given two revelations of truth—nature and Scripture. See Romans 1:19-20; Psalm 19:1-4; Isaiah 40:26; Romans 10:17; John 20:31; Acts 17:24-31; and John 1:1-5. If these two seem contradictory it is because one has been misunderstood—and that is a clue to all that will follow in this book.

The unplumbed depths of Genesis 1:1 will amaze even the scientist. Time, space, force, and substance are all found here. It is the acorn of all else, including the answers to our many questions.

We have only touched upon the most important feature of Genesis 1:1. Here at the Bible's opening the first subject introduced is *God*. The Hebrew word used will occur 2,570 times in the book that follows. The priority given to the Creator assures us that he is the one great circumstance of life,a1a1a1a1a1a1a1a1a1a1a1a1a1 and that all other circumstances affecting those who believe in him are necessarily the wisest, kindest, and best.
Belief in God is either a fact like sand, or a fantasy like Santa. This belief may be right or wrong, but never say that it is trivial. According to Mortimer Adler, the genius behind *The Great Books of the Western World*, it is the greatest and most influential idea that

has ever entered the human mind. Measure it against all other revolutionary ideas of history—control of fire, the wheel, the ship, symphonic orchestras, and anaesthetics. Now compare with these the idea of God, which teaches us that life has meaning because an all-wise, all-powerful, all-loving being wished to share his untold wealth with creatures like us.

The idea of God has guided more lives, changed more history, and inspired more music, poetry, and philosophy than any other idea ever. And it determines how you and I think and act. G. K. Chesterton said that a landlady should not enquire of a new lodger whether he has money. She should ask him what he believes about God.

God is the most loaded of all concepts. None other has been so mauled and soiled. It is attended by a host of vested interests—on both sides. Aldous Huxley and his brother Julian said they had excellent reasons for not believing in God—they did not want to be trammelled by morals, especially in the sexual arena. Millions have made money, even become wealthy, because of the way they have misused this belief. Others have died for it, by the thousands. The only other idea that can protect it is the Incarnation. If God is like Christ we are sheltered from misconceptions. But if there had never been the Bethlehem event we could not be certain whether God is good or evil, whether he is for us or against us. As cold is the absence of heat, and darkness the absence of light, so evil is the absence of God.

God is mentioned thirty-five times in the opening record of the Bible. Genesis chapter 1 is not about science or wealth but about God. After reading this chapter we must decide whether God matters tremendously or whether he matters at all. It depends on our attitude to this revelation. If he is meant to be in our lives what the sun is to the solar system, dwarfing all else, we have a challenge which if accepted guarantees all else. If we choose to live as though God is not, we invite catastrophe and eternal loss.

Genesis was written for a world which, except for the Jews, feared "gods." Eons of superstition had blinded beings made in the divine image, and the result was always days with menacing shadows. Now God is saying: "Let there be light," in order that the shadows might flee away. To know God as he is, guarantees that we will love and trust him in all circumstances. *All other knowledge is chaff compared with that.*

Observe what Genesis 1 is saying about human beings. They have value. Their lives have meaning, a meaning that can be glorious and eternal. Important though Genesis 1:26 is concerning man's creation, the following verses supersede it, for the Sabbath there introduced is a figure both of the gospel and eternity. *Man is more than the beasts. He has capacity for worship and can live forever if he rests in God.* This unique gift from God is a parable of the contentment we have when we rest in the finished work of Christ on the Cross. It is also a symbol of the new heavens and the new earth where we will rest from all the sorrows and trials of this present life. The Sabbath regularly reminds us of the essence of protology (the study of the first things) and eschatology (the study of the last things) as well as the everlasting gospel. See Hebrews 4:3 and 9.

Where there is no God there is no man, no meaning, no hope, no forgiveness, and no eternal life. Listen! Listen! All passion is out of place in a universe devoid of God. There is nothing to live for, and nothing to die for. But if we were only animals such thoughts could never enter our heads!

Those who reject the Bible on the basis of science—Genesis in particular—are usually asking us to believe the following impossible things:

> Nothing produced everything.
> Non-life produced life.
> Randomness produced fine-tuning.
> Chaos produced information.
> Unconsciousness produced consciousness.
> Non-reason produced reason.

CHAPTER TWO SUMMARY:

"In the beginning, God created heaven and earth."

Genesis 1:1 is the most important sentence ever written or spoken. It comprehends time, space, substance and power—the basic parameters known to science. It refutes the errors that have destroyed millions: atheism, agnosticism, materialism, polytheism, pantheism, dualism, humanism, astrology, the eternity of matter, and the philosophy of eternal recurrence, etc.

If any of us had a millennium to think up a better opening sentence for the Bible we could not do it. It tells us that we are not alone and that life has meaning. Without this sentence there would be no reason for life, for distinguishing between good and evil, for making judgments about better or worse, for rejoicing in faith, hope, and love. We are not "meaningless clots of coincidental molecules"—we are the children of a loving heavenly Father.

Never forget this: Genesis 1 is a table of contents for the whole Bible. It begins with God, the Spirit, and the Word of God. See 1 John 3:23,24 for the combination of God's word (his commands), the Father, the Son, and the Spirit. See also 1 John 1:1-3; John 1:1-5.

Genesis 1:2 presents us with the symbols of sin—darkness and chaos. Next the light of God's Word is followed by resurrection (see verses 3 and 9). Then we have the account of a new creation, which as Spurgeon and many others have seen, is typical also of conversion. See 2 Corinthians 5: 17.

Finally, as the Word continues to be spoken, and the Spirit continues to move, we see man in the image of God entering his rest. That rest pointed to the tomb rest at Calvary and the glorious rest of the new creation in Revelation chapters 21 and 22. The word "finished" in Genesis 2:1 points to John 19:30 and Revelation 10:7 and 20:5.

Chapter Three

Genesis and the Fight of Faith

THE FIGHT OF faith referred to by the Apostle Paul consists in keeping prominent in all our thinking the reality and nature of our heavenly Father, the Creator, Redeemer, and Judge of all. We must not be intimidated by life's trials or its challenges and conundrums. Beware of false arguments such as those urged by those scientists committed to unbelief. Repeatedly, it is said that all of humanity is only a worthless microscopic dot when measured by the immensity of the universe. This argument is false. *Size does not determine significance.* What is a mountain of mud compared to a handful of diamonds? The universe would be only a rubbish heap if it did not include humans—us—who can think, reason, choose and do. Shakespeare had it right when he declared about man:

> How noble in reason, how infinite in faculties, in form and moving, how express and admirable in action, how like an angel in apprehension, how like a God! The beauty of the world; the paragon of animals.
> *Hamlet*

William Paley used his faculties for the subsequent blessing of millions. He proposed the famous watch argument. If in wandering across a desert I stumbled upon an unexpected artifact such as a watch, what would I conclude? The watch is entirely different to the stones over which I have passed. It shows human contrivance as its source. Through much of the twentieth century, unbelievers ridiculed Paley, but with the advent of the Anthropic Principle all this changed. As Michael Denton has pointed out, Paley now has remounted his throne. We adorn this chapter with some words from Paley, "True fortitude of understanding consists in not suffering what we know to be disturbed by what we do not know."[1]

As we venture into realms where certainty is not always possible, that advice can be salutary.

In every practical decision of life we choose on the basis of the weight of evidence. It is never the case that the truths we seek are entirely luminous and with no blunt edges or ambiguity. As we fight life's battles the suspicion that our efforts are needless and useless is weakening and leads to failure and distress. Consider the verdict on life offered by Philip Adams:

> We are as significant as the eighth[sic]-billionth grain of sand beyond the final palm tree in the most distant oasis in the Sahara. "Believe it or not," *Australian Weekend Review,* 25-26 January 1997, page 2

Morris West, we think, was more thoughtful and sane:

> The strongest compulsion to belief is not reason, but need. We cannot endure to live in a mad universe. We are compelled for our own sanity, to make sense of it. Sooner or later we are forced either to blaspheme or to pursue the pilgrim search for the source of light—the shine where creative love resides. *A View from the Ridge: the Testimony of a Pilgrim,* page 9

But even Morris has missed the ultimate reason for our faith. It is the supernatural influence of the Holy Spirit upon the open mind that reveals Christ and bestows a certainty of conviction to which reason could not attain. See John 16:7-11:

> [7] But very truly I tell you, it is for your good that I am going away. Unless I go away, the Advocate will not come to you; but if I go, I will send him to you. [8] When he comes he will prove the world to be in the wrong about sin and righteousness and judgment; [9] about sin, because people do not believe in me; [10]

---

1   Later in this manuscript we consider David Hume's objections to the design argument. See comments in *The Mystery of Language,* and those linked with Dembski's books.

about righteousness, because I am going to the Father, where you can see me no longer; [11] and about judgment, because the prince of this world now stands condemned.

Chapter Three Summary:

Hebrews 11:1 says that by faith we believe that God created the world. But faith is not credulity. There is abundant evidence for it. Even science is based on faith—faith that our senses are not betraying us when we appraise and measure and record, faith that there is a world beyond the messages given by our brains.

We make all decisions on a weight of evidence, and 100 times a day we make choices based on incomplete evidence. To have absolute proof of any thing real there would have to be perfect measuring instruments, an infinite number of observations, and perfect judgment without any tinge of bias. If God came down over our city and recited the Ten Commandments every night our obedience would not come from loving faith but from fear.

The sublimity of Genesis chapter one gives us glad assurance that life is meaningful and that the fight of faith is worthwhile.

CHAPTER FOUR

The seal of seven

THE BIBLE IS quite unlike any other book in a hundred ways. And Genesis shares in this distinction. Compared with the writings of Plato, Aristotle, or other famous writers it stands out as unique. There are ancient Sumerian and Egyptian writings with creation myths, but they are filled with absurdities. *Just as the teachings of Christ are authenticated by their freedom from contemporary falsities so it is with the Bible's first book.*

There is a marvellous precision in Genesis 1. It is characterized by what some have called "the seal of seven." The first sentence has seven Hebrew words and four times seven Hebrew letters. The three nouns: "God," "heaven," and "earth" have a combined numeric value of 777. (Each Hebrew letter stands for a number—see any Hebrew Grammar). There is a Hebrew verb "created," and its numeric value is 203—seven times twenty-nine. According to some researchers there are at least thirty different numeric features in this verse. Statistically, if this is true, the chance of it happening is one in thirty million. I have checked out at least a dozen of these numerical factors from my Hebrew Bible, but I do not endorse the extreme views of Ivan Panin, who "'proves' the authenticity of the Bible by the mathematical seal beneath its surface."

The second verse of Genesis chapter 1 has seven times two words, and the last paragraph of the creation account (Genesis 2:1-3) is constructed similarly, including three statements of seven Hebrew words each with the word for seventh in the centre.

The first genealogy in the Bible is the genealogy of the heavens and the earth and it is divided into seven divisions. The next genealogy is found at the end of Genesis 4 and has seven names. The seventh man in this genealogy is Lamech. He utters an oath embracing the number seven three times. The years of the later Lamech (Genesis 5) are 777.

Genesis 2:4–4:26 is a complete unit in itself. When we study Genesis 4 in this setting, again the number seven strikes us repeatedly in one form or another (sometimes multiples of seven like fourteen or thirty-five). See particularly verses 15 and 24. Key words in this passage occur either seven times or a multiple of seven. In 4:1-17 "Abel" and "brother" occur seven times. Cain is mentioned twice seven times = fourteen. Counting in the whole unit (2:4-4:26) "earth" occurs seven times, "land" fourteen times, and "God," "the Lord," or "the Lord God" thirty-five times (five times seven). This last reckoning matches precisely the thirty-five uses of "God" in the first unit (1:1–2:3). When we come to the concluding verse (4:26), we have the seventieth reference to God in Genesis so far, and "call" or "called" appears for the fourteenth time. A number of scholars have stressed this anomaly. See the commentaries by Wenham and Cassuto for examples.

Now it may be that you are not impressed by passages with this phenomenon—verbal mosaics stamped with the Bible's special number, seven. So try writing several pages duplicating what Genesis does. If what you accomplish makes sense then you have something to boast about for it just does not come easily.

The next genealogy is Genesis 5, and here the seventh man is so close to God he does not die but is taken to heaven for eternal rapturous rest. The numbers in this chapter are based on the Babylonian sexagesimal system (sixties); each given age is a multiple of five years equalling sixty months. Wherever there is an exception to this, it is because a seven has been added. The total ages of the antediluvians come to 8,575, which is seven times 1,225. The ages from the Flood to Abraham add up to 2,996, which is also a multiple of seven. In Genesis 46:8, the sons of Jacob are listed. The seventh son is Gad (whose numeric number from the Hebrew letters of his name is seven), and he has seven sons. Genesis 46:27 states that seventy people went into Egypt.

All of this reminds us of the first New Testament genealogies. Matthew has three lots of fourteen in chapter 1; i.e. three lots of seven times two. Luke has seventy-seven generations. His whole book revolves around several pericopes, beginning each time with reference to the seventh-day Sabbath. (Most of this information can be found in such learned volumes as Umberto Cassuto's *Commentary on the Pentateuch*, part one, L. R. Bailey's *Genesis, Creation, and Creationism*, and Gordon Wenham's Commentary on Genesis.)

Let it not be missed that there are *seven* chief saints in Genesis, and they typify the biography and pilgrimage of every Christian. Study these: Adam: the life of sin; Abel: the life of worship and conflict: Noah: the life of salvation: Abraham: the life of faith: Isaac: the life of sonship: Jacob: the life of service: Joseph: the life of suffering with glory to follow. Like the Beatitudes, these set forth the stages of the believer's experience.

In 1 Kings 6:7 we read that "in building the temple, only blocks dressed at the quarry were used, and no hammer, chisel, or any other iron tool was heard at the temple site while it was being built." This is a fit picture of how the Bible came together. There was one divine Architect of the revelation of truth but the builders of the biblical temple were many.

As the twenty-six letters of the alphabet could not compose *Hamlet* without the mind of Shakespeare, as the seven notes of the octave needed Handel to create the *Hallelujah Chorus*, so the elements of our universe needed the Creator to produce the glories of our present home and the one to come. "The universe is concrete music. It is a song of which God is the singer; a poem with stars for syllables, and the measureless forces that rush through space for melody" (W. H. Fitchett, *The Beliefs of Unbelief*, page 35).

Genesis reminds us: choose between these three: an Eternal Nothing which brought forth both mind and matter; Eternal Matter which created mind; or an Eternal Mind which originated all things. As Fitchett has commented:

> The first assumption is inconceivable; the second is impossible and absurd; the third is the only theory in which the sane mind

can finally rest. And it is the creed of Christianity! 'Belief in God is the first instinct, and the last conviction, of sane intelligence.' *Ibid.*, page 37

The same writer stirs us with these words:

> What conception can be more terrifying to the imagination than that of a mindless universe! We are passengers in a train rushing at maddest speed, but whither we cannot tell. There are no signals on this line; no engineer has laid the rails; no driver is on the footplate. Happiness, for us, depends on the presence of certain qualities in the universe—love, foresight, justice, and righteousness. But these are personal qualities; and since there is no personal God these things are not to be found in the system to which we belong. We are an orphan race, wandering under pitiless and empty skies. ...
>
> A race with a mindless universe about it, a hopeless grave beneath it, and empty heavens above it. What would happen in such a world? Prayer would die, and all the forces which go with prayer. Worship would fall silent. The great charities born of religion would perish. Grief could have no comfort, mystery no explanation, truth no necessary sacredness, loss no compensating equity. *Ibid.*, pages 54, 60

Genesis exists to save us from the midnight chaos of such a hell. Our Creator has an infinite Mind and a depthless Heart.

CHAPTER FOUR SUMMARY:

God is the divine Mathematician as believing scientists have testified for centuries. The early chapters of Genesis reveal intricate mathematical patterns beyond human devising. Genesis 1:1 contains seven Hebrew words and four times seven Hebrew letters. The three nouns, God, heavens, earth have a combined value of 777. Every Hebrew letter stands for a number—*Gematria*. The Hebrew word for "created" has a numeric value of seven times twenty-nine—203. According to some researchers there are at least thirty different numeric features in this verse. Statistically, if this is true, the chance of it happening is one in thirty million.

The next sentence has twice as many Hebrew words, seven times two, and the last paragraph of the creation account (Genesis 2:1-3) is constructed similarly, including three statements of seven Hebrew words each, with the word for seventh in the centre.

Genesis forces us to make a choice: An eternal nothing which made matter and mind; eternal matter which made mind; or an eternal Mind which created matter and mind. The first is inconceivable, the second impossible and absurd, but we can rest in the third.

Chapter Five

The gospel pattern through Genesis and beyond

The gospel in Genesis chapters 1–3

Genesis is the seed-plot of the Bible. All its themes keep recurring throughout Scripture. All the sixty-six books take for granted that God is the Creator of everything and that humans were made in his spiritual image.

> Creation means that God is the true home of man's spirit. When man loses this knowledge he is a lost man. Unable to take bearings to determine where he is, or where he shall go, he knows not who he is. Estranged from his father, he is a stranger to himself. (*Christianity Today*, 5 January 1962)

> The doctrine of creation is basic to the Christian faith. It is so basic that neither the cross nor the resurrection has meaning without it, for Calvary meant the end of the old creation and the Resurrection the beginning of the new. The prodigal son came to himself when he remembered his father.
> *Ibid.*

Redemption is a new creation (2 Cor. 5:17). So the burden of the Bible from Genesis to Revelation is to show the need and manner of this new creation. Therefore Christ, the Creator, is ever central. No wonder we read that after his resurrection "beginning with Moses and all the prophets, he interpreted to them in all the Scriptures the things concerning himself" (Luke 24:27). On an earlier occasion he had said: "Moses wrote of me" (John 5:46).

Spurgeon loved to show how the gospel was to be found throughout the Old Testament. In speaking on 2 Corinthians 5:17 he illustrated his theme by drawing from Genesis chapter 1. Here are his words:

> We must note that if any man be in Christ he is a new creature, and the creation of him bears some resemblance to the creation of the world. ... that wonderful first chapter of Genesis is a Bible in miniature. ... Behold, by nature we lie like chaos; a mass of disorder, confusion, and darkness. As in the old creation so in the new, the Spirit of God broodeth over us and moveth upon the face of all things. Then the word of the Lord comes and says within us, as aforetime in chaos and old night, 'let there be light' and there is light. After light there comes a division of the light from the darkness, and we learn to call them by their names. The light is 'day' and the darkness is 'night.' So to us there is a knowing and naming of things, and a discerning of difference in matters which before we confounded when we put light for darkness. After a while there cometh forth in us the lower forms of spiritual life. As in the earth there came grasses and herbs, so in us there come desire, hope, and sorrow for sin. By-and-by there appears on the globe fowl and fish, and beasts, and living things, and life beyond all count. So also in the new creation, from having life we go on to have it more abundantly. God by degrees created all his works, till at last he had finished all the host of them, and even so he works on till he completes in us the new creation and looks upon us with rejoicing. Then he bringeth to us a day of rest, blessing us and causing us to enter into his rest because of his finished work
> *The Metropolitan Tabernacle Pulpit*, Vol. 22, pages 691-692

Not only people and events, but the created beauties of nature testify of Christ.

> I see his blood upon the rose,
> And in the stars the glory of his eyes.
> His body gleams amid eternal snows,
> His tears fall from the sky.
> I see his face in every flower
> The thunder and the singing of the birds are but his voice.
> And carved by his power the rocks are his written words.
> All pathways by his feet were worn,

His strong heart stirs the ever-beating sea,
His crown of thorns is twined with every thorn
His cross is every tree
(Joseph Mary Plunkett)

As soon as Scripture opens we find the symbols of death and resurrection (chaos, darkness, and then light, and on the third day the rising up of the earth from the threatening waters) and the moving of the life-giving Spirit. The same themes occur intensified at the end of each of the four Gospels and again at the end of the Bible in Revelation chapter 20.

At the close of the creation account we read of the hallowing not of a place or a person but of time. The Sabbath of the seventh day has many layers of meaning, but chief among these is the promised rest of heart and conscience to all who have been created anew. No wonder the fourth commandment is alluded to about 150 times.

Genesis 2, with its sketch of Paradise, makes much of living waters. This, too, will find constant repetition in Scripture. See Exodus 17, Ezekiel 47, John chapters 4 and 7, and Revelation 22. Both the second and third chapters of Genesis have allusions to the sanctuary and temples to be enlarged upon in later books. The precious stones, the gold, the water, the cherubim—all meet us again in the account in Exodus of the sanctuary. The onyx stone was used for the high priestly garments and for decorating the tabernacle and the temple (Ex. 25:7; 1 Chr. 29:2; Ex. 28:9-14). Gold was used for covering the sacred furniture such as the ark.

God is the creator and lover of the beautiful, and worship, true worship, alone can give us moral beauty and keep us in Paradise. And this worship is ever cleansing and invigorating. It is linked to the hallowed Sabbath of Genesis 2:1-3, and should regularly follow work. Genesis 2:15 makes it clear that there can be no lasting happiness without fulfilling work.

Do not minimize the importance of the symbolism in Genesis— here in chapter two we have symbols about the blessed verities of life—worship, work and rest, beauty, cleansing and refreshing, the loving fellowship between husband and wife, food, and the testing of temptation. How marvellously comprehensive is Scripture!

Wenham suggests that the account of Eden is another illustration of the way in which Genesis stoops to use some mythological beliefs but transforms them. Mesopotamian mythology had a Paradise at the northern end of what we know as the Persian Gulf. Paradise is referred to three times in Scripture—Luke 23:43; 2 Corinthians 12:4; and Revelation 2:7. Christ used the term in his dying agonies. Many elements of reality somehow reached the pagan world, although almost always distorted.

The institution of marriage is used throughout the Bible as an emblem of the loving relationship between Christ and every believer. See Ephesians 5:22-32. In Genesis 2:23 Adam sings when he is given his bride. He is in love. Wenham points out that Adam's poetry employs many of the standard techniques of Hebrew poetry: parallelism, assonance and word play, chiasmus, and verbal repetition. Verse 24 shows that there is a leaving before a cleaving. These are not Adam's words, but the narrator's. Christ quoted this in Matthew 19:5. The Song of Solomon devotes eight chapters to enlarging and beautifying this original paradigm of human love.

Within a very brief space Genesis 2 has told us much about the nature of life as God appointed it. It ever gives God priority (2:1-3) with emphasis on complete obedience (vv. 16,17). It includes service (v. 15) and human love (vv. 23-25) and dwelling amidst nature's prodigal gifts and beauty.

This chapter sets forth the two institutions that are the hinges of the Decalogue and society. Worship (the Sabbath) and marriage underlie every command of the Decalogue but particularly the fourth and fifth. When these are neglected, as in our contemporary world, society begins to wither and die.

Apart from the references to gold and precious stones in chapter 2, which point to the furnishings of the Tabernacle illustrating the way of salvation, trees next are prominent (Gen. 2:16,17). Repeatedly, the New Testament tells us that Christ suffered on a tree. See Galatians

3:13; 1 Peter 2:24; Acts 5:30, 10:39; 13:29. Every tree is meant to remind us of the Cross.

The first tree was planted by God (see Genesis 2:9). But the second tree, that of the Cross, was planted by sinful men (Matt. 27:35). The first tree was "pleasant to the eyes" (3:6), but the second tree with its gore, taunting men, darkness, and agony was repellent. "They saw in him no beauty that they should desire him" (Isa. 53:2). God forbade man to eat of the first tree (Gen. 2:17). But we are invited to eat of the second. "Taste and see that the Lord is good."

See John 6:50-58. Because God forbade the eating from the first tree Satan did all he could to seduce our first parents into eating the forbidden fruit. But as regards the second tree, Satan does all he can to prevent us eating of it. The eating of the first tree brought sin and death, but to eat of the second brings everlasting life. Adam became a thief and was ejected from Paradise. Another thief at the Cross by faith was promised Paradise.

As Arthur Pink points out in *Gleanings in Genesis* (from which I am drawing) there are also points of resemblance. Both trees were planted in a garden. See John 19:41. In connection with both trees we find the words "in the midst" (Gen. 2:9 and John 19:18). This is to remind us of the centrality of Christ and his sacrifice. The Savior of Calvary stands between God and man, between the Father and the Spirit, between life and death, between time and eternity, law and grace, judgment and mercy. To find Christ as our center is to find Paradise. Only if we keep him in the center of all our beliefs and practices can all be well.

Both the testing tree of Eden and the testing tree of Calvary are trees of the knowledge of good and evil. Only at Calvary do we see the depths of sin and the miracle of grace. When we are converted, then Calvary becomes to us "pleasant to the eyes, good for food, a tree to be desired to make one wise."

John stresses the garden in which the Crucifixion took place because a garden is a place of life and death. Seeds are sown, buried, but spring to life again as in resurrection. John is telling us that Christ will rise again. See John 19:41. Surely this is worthy of much reflection. *Never think that the account of Genesis 3 is a thoughtless myth—it is an inspired preview of that later garden where Adam's sin was atoned for.* (Gethsemane and the Cross belong together; both are said to be in a garden.)

John seems to mention the garden casually, but his allusion is of very great significance. Consider, at Calvary, where we have the Cross, which was both a tree of life and a tree of the knowledge of good and evil (the goodness of God and the evil of sin and Satan), we have two thieves at the trees (like Adam and Eve in Eden), we have the silent Mary representing all womankind and symbolizing also the penitence of Eve. Mary is speechless while it was Eve's words that unleashed the avalanche of sin. Satan, the serpent, is also at Calvary speaking now through the throats of Pharisees. "He saved others, himself he cannot save" (Matt. 27:42).

Consider also how Christ in the Gospels is represented as bearing at Golgotha all the marks of the penalty proscribed in Eden. In Eden we have these seven features: God's curse, nakedness, thorns, sorrow, sweat, separation (cast out of Eden), and the sword (death). Think now on the antitype: Christ is made a curse for us (Gal. 3:13); he is naked on the Cross, he wears the crown of thorns, in Gethsemane (which is part of the Atonement) he sweats blood; he is here the Man of Sorrows foretold by Isaiah 53:3; God separates from him ("My God, my God, why hast thou forsaken me?"); and finally he endures sin's penalty of death (represented by the drawn sword of the cherubim in Eden). Yet none of the evangelists invite us to compare this climactic tragedy with Genesis chapter 3.

The replay is all of the inspiring Spirit and part of the actual history of Calvary. When we understand how the Fall in Eden and the Atonement of Calvary fit together like key and lock we shall never again doubt the historicity of Genesis 3 and its deep theological importance, despite its obvious symbolism. This should guide us as we consider later chapters in this first section of Genesis, which contain so much beyond human invention.

Calvary and the Atonement are further prefigured in verse 21:

"The Lord God made garments of skins for Adam and his wife, and clothed them." These words are the seed from which the four Gospels and the book of Romans spring. The symbolic act of God taught our first parents that no covering ourselves by our own efforts is acceptable to Heaven. Any figleaf garment of our own self-righteousness must be surrendered. Our covering must come from God, and it can be provided only through the death of another. Here is the gospel principle of substitution. We deserve to die, but Another has taken our place and discharged our debt by his own sacrifice. The coats of skins and the trees of this chapter are depthless in meaning.

In Genesis 18 Abraham's celestial visitors find rest under the tree, as we are all intended to do. There is no other place to find rest than the Cross. In Exodus 15 the branch of a tree transforms bitter waters to sweet as does meditation on Calvary. In 2 Kings 6 the branch resurrects the lost. The order is significant. In Genesis 3 the tree becomes the place of the curse, but in the eighteenth chapter it is the place of rest. In Exodus 15 the tree has transforming power for all the trying events of life, and in 2 Kings 6 we learn that this includes resurrection from death.

Trees are places of rest and beauty. They offer food and shelter. They have in themselves the seed of continued life. *In all these ways every good tree points to the Cross of Christ.* Thus the earliest references to trees in Scripture, Genesis chapters 2, 3, and 18, put together with the following references in Exodus 15 and 2 Kings 6, give us the gospel. They assure us that Calvary tests our hearts, but offers rest, sweetness and resurrection power if our faith is riveted to the Savior of the Cross.

We have made much of Genesis 3 because it is the foundation on which the rest of Scripture is built. Because of the rebellion (the "Fall") in Eden, mankind needed a Savior. If there was no Fall, the rest of the Bible is redundant. Many thoughtful writers have told us that the doctrine of Original Sin is one that needs no argumentative substantiation. Its factuality is too obvious.

CHAPTER FIVE SUMMARY:

Genesis is the seed-plot of Scripture. All its themes keep recurring throughout the whole Bible. And all sixty-six books take for granted that God is the creator of everything and also our preserver and eedeemer.

Redemption itself is a new creation (2 Cor. 5:17). The everlasting gospel at the heart of Christianity is found in every book of the Bible. We are saved by faith alone, but the faith that saves is never alone. We are not saved by faith plus works, but by a faith that works. It does not matter who we are, but whose we are.

2 Corinthians 5:14-21 says it all. See especially verse 14: "If one died for all, then all died." When Christ died as our Representative, God counted it that we all died—we have paid for all our sins of yesterday, today and tomorrow.

Each chapter of Genesis has infinite depths. The institutions of Genesis 2—the Sabbath and marriage—image the gospel. Physical rest on the holy day symbolizes the rest of heart we have when we trust in Christ's finished work. Marriage with its love and union pictures the relationship between Christ and the church invisible. The mystical trees and serpent in Genesis 3 point to the marvels of the Atonement on Calvary.

Repeatedly, the New Testament calls the Cross a "tree." It is both a tree of life, and a tree of the knowledge of good and evil. The seven marks of the curse in Genesis 3 reoccur at Golgotha: curse, nakedness, thorns, sorrow, sweat, separation, and the sword (death). It is not by chance that John 19:41 tells us that where Christ died there was a garden—the place of death and resurrection and the antitype of the site of the Fall in Eden.

Chapter Six

Calvary prefigured

IN GENESIS CHAPTER 2 Adam's side is opened on the sixth day so that he might have a bride, and our Lord likewise had his side opened on the sixth day of Passion Week, so that we, the church, might be his bride. That which came from Adam's side made his bride, and the blood and water from the side of Christ on the Cross prefigured justification and sanctification.

In Genesis 3 we learn that refusing to believe in the love of God and disobeying his word brings death. In this chapter the avalanche of sin is launched. But we learn also of the loving Redeemer who will fight with the serpent (Satan) though bruised to death in the process. All the sorrow and curse of sin is to be eradicated with the coming of a Redeemer. But Genesis 3:15 also tells us that there is to be continuing conflict between the seed of the serpent and the seed of the woman, prefiguring the lost and the saved. Note that *this first prophecy encapsulates the whole gospel as an oak lies in its acorn.* The virgin birth and incarnation are here, as are all Christ's sorrows from Bethlehem to Calvary, the defeat of Satan, the two kingdoms and two societies, and the ultimate glory after the ministry of the last Pentecost.

In Genesis 4 we read of the Good Shepherd who died young because of the envy and hatred of his brother. This was the beginning of the bruising of the woman's seed, which was to climax at Golgotha. And yet that bruising ultimately destroyed our great Adversary (see Romans 16:20).

Here we have the first of a series of narratives that teach what Christ taught Nicodemus. Unless a person is born again, he or she can never see the kingdom of Heaven (John 3:3). Repeatedly in Genesis we are told about sets of brothers different in character and destiny.

Cain and Abel, Ishmael and Isaac, Esau and Jacob (Jacob's many sons contrasted with Joseph similarly). In each instance the firstborn is carnally-minded while the secondborn becomes a model of the spirit-filled follower of Christ. The same lesson is taught by the first two generations of Israel. The first died in the desert after forty years of rebellion, the second generation by faith entered the Promised Land. Again, consider the first kings of Israel, Saul and David. Saul, though outwardly impressive and multi-gifted, proves carnal and kills himself. David, the second king, despite his failures, is a man after God's own heart.

So in the first set of brothers presented to us in Scripture, Cain the firstborn is carnal. According to the Hebrew his name signifies a lance or spear—a murder weapon. While Abel is a good shepherd and follows the model of Genesis 3:21, depending upon the blood of a substitute, Cain refuses to follow the divine pattern. At the time of the Exodus only those houses with the sign of the blood of a lamb were sheltered when judgment marched through the land. Romans 3:25 explains this when speaking of Christ, saying: "God presented him as a sacrifice of atonement, through faith in his blood." Until our conversion God views us as carnal and lost. Our firstborn nature is without the indwelling Spirit and is actually "dead." We must be born again (1 Corinthians 15:46).

The murder of Abel, as mentioned, points to the Cross. Cain, the murderer of the good shepherd was young like Christ at Calvary. He typifies not only all the firstborn lacking regeneration, but also the Jewish people who for envy surrendered their Brother to death. The Jews after Calvary would follow the course of Cain. They, too, have continued to reject the blood sacrifice. They, too, have become wanderers and fugitives (see Deuteronomy 28:65). They, too, have been constantly in dread of non-Jews who so often have persecuted them cruelly. They, like Cain, have chiefly dwelled in cities. But they are "beloved for the fathers' sake" (Romans 11:28, KJV).

The names of the righteous seed given in the next chapter spell out the whole gospel as one of the early Protestant Reformers discovered.

Adam	Man,
Seth	Appointed,
Enos	Wretched, fallen man,
Canaan	Lamenting;
Mahalaleel	The Blessed God,
Jared	Shall descend,
Enoch	Teaching, dedicated, disciplined,
Methuselah	His death shall bring,
Lamech	Power,
Noah	Rest and comfort.

The Reformer Ursinus, author of the Heidelberg Catechism, is credited with discovering this. The meaning of some of the names is disputed, but the weight of evidence for most supports the meanings Ursinus assigned.

Three names stand out: Adam, Enoch, and Noah. Adam brought us life and death. Enoch shows us the way to live in time and eternity—he walked with God. Noah tells us that even in times of crisis we may find rest and comfort. Enoch's translation was the promise that death would not reign forever. In the patriarchal era Enoch cheated death and went home to glory. In the Jewish era Elijah had the same experience. In our Christian age, as 1 Thessalonians 4 tells us, those who are alive at the coming of the Lord will go to heaven with him without experiencing death. "O grave, where is thy victory? O death, where is thy sting?"

In Noah we find a man whose righteousness led to the salvation of his family. God could say "Thee only have I seen righteous," but the family was invited to avoid the coming catastrophe. The hero of the Flood typified our Lord in several ways: he was the first person to be called "just" in Genesis though others were also. We are told he was "perfect in his generation"—this reminds us of the immaculate humanity of Christ. We are told that Noah "walked with God" (Gen. 6:9). He did a mighty work and he did it alone—we are not told of any helpers. The animal creation was subject to him—compare Mark 1:13. He becomes the Savior of those who believed and exemplified faith for he had never seen a flood. His faith was conjoined with obedience. See Hebrews 11:7 and Genesis 6:22. Furthermore, we are told that God established his covenant with Noah (Gen. 9:8,9). Compare Hebrews 13:20. The Hebrew word translated "go" in Genesis 7:1 (go into the ark) in some recent versions is translated "come" in the KJV. The original term can mean either. We prefer "come" for this suggests God was with him in the ark that was to be so brutally assaulted by nature. It is the first of 500 references to the word "come," and it is for each of us to accept the invitation and to find in Christ our ark, our refuge from the storms of life and death.

The ark also was a remarkable type of Christ. It was God's provision for salvation and he graciously revealed it to the one man who trusted him. It was made of gopher wood (Gen. 6:14). This meant trees had to be cut down. The death of trees led to life for Noah and his family. The death on the Tree of Calvary brings life to us. It was a place of absolute security and a refuge from judgment. Note that, "the Lord shut him in" (Gen. 7:16). Noah did not have to take care of himself. Once he entered the ark the Lord would care for him. There was only one door—compare John 10:10 and John 14:6. The ark had also one window (Gen. 6:16). Repeatedly, Scripture admonishes us to look up for only so can we walk by faith (Col. 3:2). Genesis 6:14 remains important for two reasons: first, we are told of the rooms in the ark (the original word means "nests"—resting places), and, second, the ark was to be covered with pitch. The word here used is not the usual word for pitch, but it is the term translated seventy times as "to make atonement."

Finally the resurrection is typified. The seventeenth day of the seventh month is mentioned. That seventh month was later changed into the first month at the time of the first Passover, and the seventeenth day, three days after the Passover, reminds us of our Lord's time in the grave after the antitypical Passover. The actual day for Christ's resurrection was the sixteenth of the month. By the seventeenth all his living saints knew it was an established fact. The ark came to rest on a mountaintop—beautiful symbol of our Lord's ascension to heaven. I refer the reader again to Arthur Pink's *Gleanings in Genesis,* which despite some dispensational errors has much to recommend it.

Following the Flood, God appointed the rainbow as the symbol of his covenant with believers (see Genesis 9:12-16). A rainbow is a union of sunshine and shower, and God's covenant is based both on his love and his justice. There are three Old Testament symbols of the divine covenant—the Sabbath, the rainbow, and circumcision. All three have meaning for us still, but the third now applies to the circumcision of the heart (see Romans 2:29). An important thing to remember about the rainbow is that it also symbolizes a bow where the arrow has already been discharged.

In chapter ten the sacred number seven is used repeatedly. Even the number of the nations is purposely reduced to seventy. The descendants of Noah's sons are set forth in multiples of seven.

The main character in chapter ten is Nimrod whose name means "the rebel." He is a type of Antichrist, the exact opposite in every way of the true Christ. Satan himself is the ultimate and original Antichrist but his followers and representatives reflect his likeness. Deception, pride, and violence are their main characteristics, and we do well to remember the admonition of Luther that "Pope self is the chief antichrist."

Nimrod is a descendant of Ham, the least spiritual of Noah's sons. His kingdom finds its centre in Babylon. Four times the word "mighty" is associated with him—(three times in Genesis 10 and 1 Chronicles 1:10)—and we are reminded that the New Testament sets forth antichrist as working with "all power" (2 Thess. 2:9). He is a "hunter"—woe betide to all those in his way. Probably he headed the rebellion presented in Genesis 11.

In Genesis 11 we have the story of the Tower of Babel, where we are warned against every false gospel that tempts us to depend on our own wisdom and work to reach heaven. But happily the Bible records God's decision to "go down" and confound the burgeoning evil. So the true Christ would descend at the Incarnation to confound Satan's kingdom.

In Genesis 12 we find Abraham who typifies Christ "the Everlasting Father" of Isaiah 9:6. Abraham left his home and became a wanderer that he might be the father of the faithful. Even so, the Son of

God forsook heaven for the wilderness of earth. Abraham was king, priest, and prophet, to his own family, as Christ is to his. To Abraham were the great promises made and he is called "the heir of the world." In both respects he points to Christ. Abraham put Hagar and Ishmael out of his house and Christ in his gospel tells us that those who are legalistic and remain "in the flesh" cannot inherit the blessings of the covenant of grace.

The most important verse in the story of this first patriarch is in Genesis 15:6, "And Abraham believed the Lord and it was credited to him as righteousness." The Hebrew for the key words here: "believed," "credited," and "righteousness," are found in this passage for the first time. (The first usage of a topic is prophetic of later use.) They show very clearly the only way of salvation. By simple trust we find life eternal. Righteousness in its fullest sense is never within anyone of us, but it is credited, imputed, reckoned to us by the grace of God, because faith links us to our Substitute and Representative. "If one died for all, then all died" (2 Cor. 5:14). *The second look at the Cross occurs when we see that we are counted as hanging there to pay the price for all our sins of the past, present, and future. Luther rightly said, "Mine are Christ's living and dying as though I had lived his life and died his death."* As substitute, Christ took our place and paid the penalty for sin. As representative, he took us with him so that all he did might be put to our account. That is the everlasting gospel.

Faith characterizes Abraham despite human failures. He has faith in the promise of God that he would yet have a son despite his and Sarah's advanced age. After twenty-five years of believing, the son came. By faith Abraham lived in tents, but he never fails to erect his worship altars. By faith he gave Lot his choice of land in which to settle. By faith he rescued Lot and his family from their enemies. By faith he refused earthly rewards (Gen. 14:22-23). By faith he was prepared to sacrifice his only son, the son of his great love. And he is our pattern. Very important are the words about Abraham's journeying: "going on still." Nothing daunted him. He just kept on going.

In Genesis 14 we are confronted by that mysterious person Melchizedek—the king-priest of Salem. Neither his birth nor his death is recorded, and therefore he typified the Savior who belongs to eternity and who would be both a King and a Priest of the churchly Jerusalem. He blessed Abraham with bread and wine to refresh him. Compare the Gospel accounts of the Last Supper. The name of this mysterious king-priest, Melchizedek, means "king of righteousness." He is both king of righteousness and king of peace (Salem means peace), so pointing to Christ. At the Cross "mercy and truth met together, and righteousness and peace kissed each other" (Psa. 85:10).

The New Testament constantly draws upon typology—Old Testament events and predictions with more meaning than the original application. See 1 Corinthians 10:11 (orig.) and especially Hebrews and Revelation.

Genesis 16 revolves around wells of living water pointing forward to the blessings of the gospel. See especially John 4:13,14. In Genesis 17 we have the institution of circumcision as the sign of the covenant. It pointed to the circumcision of the heart for all who follow Christ. See Philippians 3:3 and Romans 2:29. In Genesis 18 Abraham becomes an intercessor and reminds us of Hebrews 7:25 about our Lord's work above.

Genesis 19 is a warning of the fate that must overtake all who spit in God's face rejecting his gifts, his love. The destruction of Sodom and Gomorrah is typical of the final burning of the world after the Last Judgment. In Genesis 20 we see the contrast between Christ and his ancient follower. Abraham sins by falsehood.

Wells of water are again brought before us in Genesis 21, but the real climax is reached in Genesis 22. In this chapter for the first time we have the words "only son," "love," and "obey." It is a preview of the Atonement. In that very precious classic *Christ in All the Scriptures* by A. M. Hodgkin, we have the following regarding Genesis 22:

> Observe that in what follows we are comparing Mount Moriah, the place of Isaac's 'sacrifice' with Mount Calvary:
>
> | | |
> |---|---|
> | Genesis 22:2 | Take thy son |
> | Hebrews 1:3 | God has spoken to us by his Son. |

35

Genesis 22:2	Thine only son
John 3:16	God gave his only begotten Son.
Genesis 22:2	Whom thou lovest
John 1:18	The only begotten Son which is in the bosom of the Father.
Genesis 22:2	And get thee into the land of Moriah.
2 Chron. 3:1	Solomon began to build the house of the Lord in Mount Moriah.
Genesis 22:2	Upon one of the mountains that I will tell thee of …
Luke 23:33	And when they were come to the place which is called Calvary *there* they crucified him.
Genesis 22:2	And offer him there for a burnt offering.
Hebrews 10:5-10	Sanctified through the body of Jesus Christ once for all.
Genesis 22:4	Abraham lifted up his eyes and saw the place afar off.
Acts 3:18	God before hath shown by the mouth of all his holy prophets that Christ should suffer. (The Father knew before the foundation of the world).
Genesis 22:6	And Abraham took the wood of the burnt offering and laid it upon Isaac his son. And they went both of them together.
John 19:17	And he, bearing his cross, went forth.
John 10:17,18	Therefore doth my Father love me, because I lay down my life. No man taketh it from me, but I lay it down of myself. This commandment have I received of my Father.

Genesis 22:7	Where is the lamb for the burnt offering?
John 1:29	Behold the lamb of God which taketh away the sin of the world.
Genesis 22:6	So they went both of them together.
Psalm 40:8	I delight to do thy will, O my God.
Genesis 22:9	Abraham built an altar there and bound Isaac his son and laid him upon the altar upon the wood.
Isaiah 53:6	The Lord hath laid on him the iniquity of us all.
Acts 2:23	Him being delivered by the determinate counsel and foreknowledge of God.
Genesis 22:10	And Abraham stretched forth his hand and took the knife to slay his son.
Isaiah 53:10	It pleased the Lord to bruise him.
Matthew 17:46	My God, my God, why hast thou forsaken me?
Genesis 22:11	The angel of the Lord called to him out of heaven
Contrast:	
Matthew 26:53,54	No voice from heaven
Matthew 27:42	He saved others, himself he cannot save.
Genesis 22:10	Thou hast not withheld thy son, thine only son.
Jeremiah 6:26	When God speaks of deep grief he compares it to the loss of an only son.
Genesis 22:13	Abraham took the ram and offered him up for a burnt offering in the stead of his son.
Isaiah 53:7,11	He is brought as a lamb to the slaughter. … He shall bear their iniquities.

| Genesis 22:8 | God will provide himself the lamb. |
| Revelation 13:8 | The lamb slain from the foundation of the world. |

In Genesis 23 we see acted out the truths that even God's saints must die, yet their dwelling place is precious. Genesis 24 tells of the work of the servant of Abraham going forth to a distant place to find a bride for the one who was, as it were, resurrected from death at Moriah. See Hebrews 11:19. Fifty days after Calvary the Holy Spirit descended on the bride that providence had provided for the Savior. See Acts chapter 2.

In Genesis 25 the barren Rebekah became a mother. It is deeply significant that the several wives emphasized in Genesis—Sarah, Rebekah, and Rachel—received their first child by miracle, prefiguring Isaiah 7:14.

In Genesis 26 verses 18-33 repeatedly speak of wells. Only when we come to the New Testament and see Christ's repeated use of the symbol of water, do we see the depth of meaning in the constant references to wells in the life of Isaac.

In Genesis 27 Jacob is portrayed to us as the type of our own first-born carnal nature, which deceives and is in turn deceived. But God does not forsake him and loves him still. So in chapter 28 Jacob is given a vision at Bethel of Christ, the ladder between heaven and earth, the go-between for all angelic ministry. Christ himself pointed to this event and its significance (see John 1:50-51). The Savior's words prove that we are not missing the way when we find him typified again and again in the Bible's first book. Never forget his words: "Moses wrote of me." See also Luke 24:25-27,44.

The most significant part of Jacob's life was his encounter with Christ on the night he feared for his life. He assumed Esau was coming to murder him. In Genesis 32:1,3 we read that angels came to encourage him. But he was still afraid. In chapter 32, from verse 22 forwards, we read of Jacob's mysterious encounter by night and the long hours of wrestling. It was a miniature of his whole life. God for so many years had been working on the heart of Jacob that he might become a new man—God's man. That night it happened. He became Israel—a prince with God. His hours of struggle in the darkness were a preview of the true Israel who agonized in Gethsemane.

We only read Genesis properly when we find Jesus there.

CHAPTER SIX SUMMARY:

Calvary and its redemption are typified throughout the chapters of Genesis. Abel, the good Shepherd who was murdered in his youth by an envious brother, foretells the betrayal and death of Christ at the hands of his Jewish brethren who envied him. Cain becomes the type of Jewry that, rejecting the blood atonement, is henceforth a wanderer and a fugitive over the centuries, hated and persecuted yet still beloved by God.

The Ark with its one door points to Christ who saves us from the wrath of God against evil. Noah, whose family is saved because of his righteousness, also typifies our Lord. Genesis 22, the story of Abraham's offering of Isaac, predicts the sacrifice of the beloved Son of God 2,000 years later at the very same place. Even the repeated references to "wells" in the story of Isaac point to him who is the well of living waters (see John 4: 13,14).

CHAPTER SEVEN

The four Gospels anticipated

WE CANNOT BYPASS *the story of Joseph, which has about 100 parallels with the Redeemer of the world.* We first see him as a despised, envied, and hated alien, innocent but falsely accused and wrongly punished. Yet he saves the lives of the enemy world with the bread of life. Apart from Arthur Pink, Ada R. Habershon is the most helpful in considering the typical significance of Joseph. See her *The Study of the Types.* Here we find about 100 comparisons between the Old Testament record and the New. I do not see how anyone studying this list could ever doubt the inspiration of both Testaments. Even some of the very words used in the first account reappear in the second. The KJV is often more accurate in this story than modern versions.

I offer just a few of these. The section at the end of this chapter details Old Testament words about Joseph that in substance reappear in the Gospels. See the source itself for the textual references.

To read all Habershon has provided with the corresponding New Testament texts is to find great spiritual wealth. Even the KJV language, which we find so difficult, has its advantages in this case as modern translators often miss the verbal parallels.

How very appropriate that the record of Joseph should come at the close of Genesis! But it should be remembered that his life is intimately connected with that of the preceding six heroes of Genesis—Adam, Abel, Noah, Abraham, Isaac, and Jacob. There is no sin recorded in the life of Joseph, and so he typifies the goal of the sanctified life.

The seven best-known saints in Genesis provide us with the biogra-

40

phy of every Christian. Adam's is the life of sin and portrays where we all start. Abel's life is one of worship and conflict as the newly converted experience the conflict of Galatians 5:17, where the flesh lusts against the spirit and vice versa (see Romans 7:14-25). Noah's is the life of salvation as he enters the ark and is saved from the Flood. Next comes Abraham who typifies the life of faith. Isaac's submission at Moriah tells us that the true Christian lives a life of sacrifice and self-denial. Jacob with his many years of service represents the walk of the Christian, and Joseph's life is one of suffering with glory to follow.

As illustrated in the earlier pages about Joseph, *all of the seven chief characters of Genesis tell us not only about our own Christian life, but also about our Savior.* Christ, like Adam, is the head of the Race. Like Adam he "slept" in order to have a bride.

Like Adam he was tempted with "the lust of the eyes, the lust of the flesh, and the pride of life" (see Matthew 4:1-10). Like Abel, Christ—the Good Shepherd—was murdered by his own because of envy. Like Noah, Christ has prepared for us a way of escape from God's wrath against sin. Becoming by conversion members of his family we are counted worthy of salvation. Like Abraham, Christ left his home to become a despised wanderer in what was only a desert land compared to Heaven. Like Isaac, Christ was a willing sacrifice, and at the very same spot—Moriah (where the Jerusalem temple was later built). Like Jacob, Christ wrestled by night in Gethsemane, and his life was one of constant service. And like Joseph—well, we have told that story.

Genesis is the first of six books, that are not only full of Christ typified and prophesied, but also replete with narratives that portray the life of every believer. Genesis is the book of sin, which records the Fall and ends with a coffin. Exodus is the book of redemption where the saved go out by the blood of the lamb. Leviticus with its many symbolic rituals is the book of worship typifying that aspect of the life of the saved. Numbers tells of the ups and downs in the wilderness, aptly portraying the Christian's experiences of sorrow and joy in this wilderness world. Deuteronomy means "the second law" and consists of a series of sermons by Moses on the borders of the Promised Land reminding the saved ones that obedience, the fruit of faith, is the way to blessing. In Joshua, led by the Man with the drawn sword, the redeemed host enter the land of milk and honey, the land of Promise—typical both of the ideal Christian life and heaven itself.

1 Corinthians 10:11 urges us to remember that the Old Testament histories typify the experiences of believers in all ages. Let us read them often that we might share the victories and avoid the defeats.

Note how the Flood is couched in the same imagery as Creation.

Creation
1. There is a pre-Creation chaos (Gen. 1:2)
2. The waters cover the earth (Gen. 1:2)
3. The Spirit overshadows the earth (Gen. 1:2)
4. The waters are divided (Gen. 1:6)
5. The dry land rises (Gen. 1:10)
6. The animals arrive (Gen. 1:24)
7. Man is made in God's likeness (Gen. 1:27)
8. Man is given dominion over the creatures and the earth (Gen. 1:28,29)

The Flood
1. There is a world chaos (Gen. 7:11)
2. The waters cover the earth (Gen. 7:19,20)
3. The wind blows on the water. (Gen 8:1)
4. The dry land is seen (Gen. 8:13,14)
5. Noah is given dominion over the creatures, and the command—first given to Adam—to subdue and populate the earth is repeated (Gen. 9:1,2)

Clearly, Genesis is not concerned with science. Its purpose is to offer salvation to lost sinners. We find further evidence for the theological bearing of Genesis when we consider how Christ is presented as the last Adam in the New Testament. He, too, has dominion over the earth—see Hebrews 2:6-9. Therefore, he could bring to the line of Peter a fish with a coin in its mouth, and he could ride the unbroken colt in Passion Week. Even the stormy waters became peaceful at his admonition. And on the Cross he wore the thorns for which the first Adam was responsible.

CHAPTER SEVEN SUMMARY

While God devoted one chapter to the record of the earth's creation he has given thirteen chapters to the story of Joseph. No sin is recorded against this final hero of Genesis and in approximately 100 ways his experience typifies the Life recorded in the four Gospels. Here was a despised alien, hated by his brethren, sold for pieces of silver to a foreign nation, falsely accused, suffering unfairly but comes out of prison to reign and saves the world with the bread of life.

Old Testament words about Joseph that in substance reappear in the Gospels

FEEDING THE FLOCK, their evil report, loved by his father, hated by his brethren, shalt thou indeed reign over us, envied, sent to his brethren, Here am I, bring me word again, he came to Shechem, wandering in the field, I seek my brethren, went after his brethren, they conspired against him, we shall see, stripped, the pit, they sat there, twenty pieces of silver, into Egypt, servant, the Lord was with Joseph, the Lord made all he did to prosper in his hand, left all in Joseph's hand, a goodly person, well favoured, how can I do this great wickedness?, whose feet they hurt with fetters, two of Pharaoh's officers in the place where Joseph was bound, I do remember my faults this day, he served them, wherefore look ye so sadly today?, think on me, show kindness, I pray thee, unto me, make mention of me, yet did not the chief butler remember Joseph, but forgot him, Here also have I done nothing that they should put me into the dungeon, out of the dungeon, the king sent and loosed him, it is not in me, a man in whom the Spirit of God is, God hath showed thee all this, none so discreet and wise, over my house, according to thy word shall all my people be ruled, without thee shall no man lift up his hand or foot, bow the knee, thirty years old.

Joseph gathered corn very much without number, Manasseh-forgetting, Ephraim-fruitful, go unto Joseph, what he says to you, do, famine over all the face of the earth, the famine waxed sore, Joseph opened all the storehouses, all countries came to buy, he it was that sold, he knew them, but they knew not him, Joseph made himself strange unto them and spoke roughly unto them, his blood is required, they knew not that Joseph understood them, he spoke unto them by an interpreter, he turned himself away from them and wept, Joseph commanded to fill their sacks with corn, to restore every man's money into his sack, to give them provision for the way, thus did he unto them, as much as they can carry, bring these men home, make ready, the men were afraid, they came near to the steward and they communed with him, other money have we brought down, Peace be to you, fear not!, they drank, and were merry with him, God hath found out the iniquity of thy servants.

Joseph made himself known, at the second time, they were troubled at his presence, I am Joseph your brother whom you sold, come near to me, God did send me, a great deliverance, Not you but God, Tarry not, there will I nourish thee, Joseph nourished all his father's household, with bread, as a little child is nourished, Behold, your eyes see that it is my mouth that speaketh unto you, you shall tell my father of all my glory, his brethren talked with him, come unto me, regard not your stuff, for the good of all the land of Egypt is yours, Joseph is yet alive, Jacob's heart fainted, for he believed them not, now let me die since I have seen thy face, my brethren, why should we die in thy presence, our money is spent, there is not ought left but our bodies, I have bought you this day, Lo, here is seed for you, and ye shall sow the land, when Joseph's brethren saw that their father was dead ... they sent a messenger unto Joseph, saying, forgive, etc. And Joseph wept. God meant it unto good ... to save much people alive. Fear ye not, and he comforted them.

Joseph is a fruitful bough whose branches run over the wall, a fruitful bough by a well, the archers have sorely grieved him, and shot at him, and hated him. His bow abode in strength and the arms of his hands were made strong by the hands of the mighty God of Jacob. From thence is the Shepherd, the stone of Israel. Let the blessing come upon the head of Joseph. Separate from his brethren. The birthright was Joseph's. Not grieved for the affliction of Joseph. A new king, who knew not Joseph. The house of Joseph shall abide in their coasts. Joshua spake unto the house of Joseph. ... Thou art a great people and hast great power. I am a great people inasmuch as the Lord hath blessed me hitherto. The hand of the house of Joseph prevailed (these last four paragraphs are summarized from Habershon).

CHAPTER 8

Moses, Christ, and the oratorio

NO ONE CAN READ Genesis without thinking of Moses as its traditional author. See T. Francis Glasson's splendid little book *Moses and the Fourth Gospel*.

Even some of Jesus' words are quoted directly from Deuteronomy. And, as Glasson points out, *all the main features of Moses' life reoccur in the Redeemer's*.

Why is this important? The parallels cited by Glasson prove that the writings of Moses, including Genesis, are not merely a straightforward record of events. *The events are shaped in the telling so that readers might see the lessons implicit in the recurrence of earlier events.* This recognition brings with it the confidence that God is in control of all events and that his people are safe in his hands. The Lord God omnipotent can be traced through chapter after chapter and becomes visible and tangible as at Bethlehem.

Spurgeon spoke so often on this theme that over a century ago a large book (*Christ in the Old Testament*) was printed reproducing his best sermons on the topic. Here is a typical quote from him:

> I will give the Old Testament to any wise man living and say, Go home and construct in your imagination an ideal character who shall exactly fit all that which is foreshadowed. Remember, he must be a prophet like unto Moses, and yet a champion like unto Joshua, he must be an Aaron and a Melchizedek; he must be both David and Solomon, Noah and Jonah, Judah and Joseph. Nay, he must not only be the lamb that was slain and the scapegoat that was not slain, the turtledove and the priest that slew the bird, but he must be the altar, the tabernacle,

46

mercy-seat and shewbread. Nay, to puzzle this wise man further, we remind him of prophecies so apparently contradictory that one would think they could never meet in one man. Such as these: 'All men shall fall down before him,' etc., and 'He is despised,' etc. He must begin by showing a man born of a virgin mother. He must be a man without spot or blemish, but one upon whom the Lord doth lay the iniquities of us all. He must be a glorious One, a Son of David, yet a root out of a dry ground. Now if the greatest intellects could set themselves to invent another key to the types and prophecies they could not do it. These wondrous hieroglyphics must be left unexplained till one comes forward and proclaims, 'The Cross of Christ and the Son of God incarnate.' Then the whole is clear, so that he who runs may read, and a child may understand.

The Biblical Illustrator, comment upon John 19:30, *John III*, pages 336-337

Billy Sunday also rejoiced in the Bible's revelation of his Savior. Notice that in his account of his pilgrimage through Scripture it is Jesus who is given first place:

Twenty-two years ago, with the Holy Spirit as my guide, I entered the temple of Christianity. I entered at the portico of Genesis, walked down through the Old Testament Art Galleries where pictures of Noah, Abraham, Moses, Joseph, Isaac, Job, and Daniel hung on the walls. I passed into the music room of Psalms, where the Spirit swept the keyboard of nature until it seemed that every reed pipe in God's great organ responded to the tuneful harp of David, the sweet singer of Israel. I entered the chamber of Ecclesiastes where the voice of the Preacher was heard and into the conservatory of Sharon and the Lily of the Valley's sweet scented spices filled and perfumed my life. I entered the business office of Proverbs and then into the observatory room of the prophets where I saw telescopes of various sizes pointed to far-off events, but all concentrated upon the Bright and Morning Star.

I entered the audience room of the King of Kings and caught a vision of his glory from the standpoint of Matthew, Mark, Luke, and John, passed into the Acts of the Apostles where the Holy Spirit was doing his work in the formation of the infant church. Then into the correspondence room where sat Paul, Peter, James, and John penning their epistles. I stepped into the throne room of Revelation where towered the glittering peaks and got a vision of the king sitting upon the throne in all his glory, and I cried 'All hail the power of Jesus name, let angels prostrate fall. Bring forth the royal diadem and crown him Lord of all.'

But what has that to do with Genesis? Simply this: Billy Sunday experienced heaven on earth and led multitudes to the Savior because he learned that everything in the Bible pointed to Jesus. And that is the way we must always read Genesis. He is the Creator, the first Adam, the tree of life, Abel, Noah and all the other saints. And by seeing him we are changed little by little into his glory.

The pattern is not always obvious but it deserves our most prayerful search. See for example the chief references to blood in Genesis beginning with the fourth chapter where blood speaks, followed by the ninth chapter where blood is sacred; then in the thirty-seventh chapter the blood is presented to the father; but chapter 42 warns us that there is a judgment associated with our reaction to the blood. In 49:22 we find that the blood cleanses. The series is completed in Exodus. In Exodus 4:9 where the blood can be a sign of God's wrath while in Exodus 12:13 it is the only covering in the time of heaven's judgments. Notice that in Exodus 12:13 *whoever* was under the blood was safe, that it was the blood and nothing but the blood which brought safety, and third, it was God's estimate of the blood that counted. How comprehensive these seven references are in setting forth the gospel of grace!

When James Mills gave up on God he wrote:

> The clouds have slowly closed in and choked all hope. Death has become only a leap in the dark, over a chasm whose rocks hold an unknown power for mangling.

But he was following the path of Cain, and the wicked of the antediluvian world. Men don't die, they suicide by forgetting their Maker, Redeemer, and Judge. Ralph Waldo Emerson once said that most of the shadows of our lives come from standing in our own sunshine. If we would but stand looking to the Sun of Righteousness who loves us infinitely, all the shadows would fall behind us. And Genesis, rightly understood, teaches this.

There are two basic convictions that permeate our thinking: the amazement that we are, and the shock that we will cease to be. These convictions are the cause of all our ultimate questions: Who are we? From whence did we come? Where are we going? How should we live? Only Genesis can answer these questions properly. Moses wrote Genesis not just for Israel, but for each of us, from chapter one to chapter fifty. He began with the living God (1:1) and closed with a coffin (a reminder of how much we need him who is "The Resurrection and the Life").

If Genesis 1 is closely studied we discover a unique sequence:

Subject	Verse(s)
Holiness	1:1
Sin	1:2 first half
The Holy Spirit	1:2 second half
The word preached	3
Light	4
Separation	4–8
Resurrection	9–10
Fruit	12–13
Shining lights	14–19
Holiness	20–31

Theodore Epp wrote on this same analogy in his book *Nuggets in Genesis,* but with much more detail using twenty-eight pages. His headings are suggestive:

At the beginning	Darkness
The first day	Light
The second day	Separation
The third day	Fruit-bearing
The fourth day	Witnessing (in this section he has sub-headings: The Sun and the Son; the

	Moon and the Church; the Stars and Christians)
The fifth day	Victorious living
The sixth day	Reigning (sub-headings: Man given dominion, conformed to God's image)

Epp could have added:	
The seventh day	Resting in the finished work of the Redeemer and Creator.

Please do not pass this by too quickly. What many writers have rightly recognized is that Genesis 1 has not only creation, but also redemption for its theme. Genesis is no ordinary book. It has heights and depths beyond all our first imaginings. Even if we live by the first four words, what a great life that would be! Christ enlarged these four words when he urged us to: "Seek first the kingdom of God and his righteousness, and all these things shall be added unto you" (Matt. 6:33).

Only when mankind gave up polytheism for monotheism was scientific progress possible. The reality of one God meant the consistency of divine laws—thus nature was unlocked. And for us as individuals *when our lives are focussed on our Maker, instead of upon a thousand trivial things, only then do we make real progress.*

CHAPTER EIGHT SUMMARY:

One cannot think long about Genesis without thinking of its traditional author—Moses. He, in scores of ways, typified Christ who also was saved from a cruel king in childhood, who also was a prophet, priest, lawgiver, and king, one willing to die for the sins of his people. The New Testament repeatedly draws from the life and words of Moses when recording the life and words of Christ. This is a vital clue for interpreting Genesis correctly. The record of the early events is so shaped as to typify what would recur long after. The purpose of Genesis is not to teach science but redemption.

Chapter Nine

Was Noah's Flood universal?

Part One: The history of interpretation

Pertinent Bible Texts:
The Lord saw how great man's wickedness on the earth had become. ... The Lord grieved that he had made man on the earth, and his heart was filled with pain. So the Lord said, 'I will wipe mankind, whom I have created, from the face of the earth—men and animals, and creatures that move along the ground, and birds of the air—for I am grieved that I have made them.'
Genesis 6:5-7

Now the earth was corrupt in God's sight and was full of violence. God saw how corrupt the earth had become, for all the people on earth had corrupted their ways. So God said to Noah, 'I am going to put an end to all people, for the earth is filled with violence because of them. I am surely going to destroy both them and the earth. So make yourself an ark.'
Genesis 6:11-14

I am going to bring floodwaters on the earth to destroy all life under the heavens, every creature that has the breath of life in it.
Genesis 6:17

You are to bring in to the ark two of all living creatures, male and female, to keep them alive with you. Two of every kind of bird, of every kind of animal and of every kind of creature that moves along the ground will come to you to be kept alive. You are to take every kind of food that is to be eaten and store it away as food for you and for them.
Genesis 6:19-21

Pairs of clean and unclean animals, of birds and of all creatures that move along the ground, male and female, came to Noah and entered the ark ... and after the seven days the floodwaters came on the earth.
Genesis 7:8-19

They had with them every wild animal according to its kind, all livestock according to their kinds, every creature that moves along the ground according to its kind, and every bird according to its kind, everything with wings. Pairs of all creatures that have the breath of life in them came to Noah and entered the ark.
Genesis 7:14-15

For forty days the flood kept coming on the earth, and as the waters increased they lifted the ark high above the earth. The waters rose and increased greatly on the earth, and the ark floated on the surface of the water. They rose greatly on the earth, and all the high mountains under the entire heavens were covered. The waters rose and covered the mountains to a depth of more than twenty feet. Every living thing that moved on the earth perished—birds, livestock, wild animals, all the creatures that swarm over the earth, and all mankind. Every living thing on the face of the earth was wiped out.
Genesis 7:17-23

The waters flooded the earth for a hundred and fifty days. But God remembered Noah ... and sent a wind over the earth, and the waters receded. Now the springs of the deep and the flood-gates of the heavens had been closed, and the rain had stopped falling from the sky. ... The waters continued to recede until the tenth month and on the first day of the tenth month the tops of the mountains became visible.
Genesis 7:24-8:5

The dove could find no place to set its feet because there was water over all the surface of the earth.
Genesis 8:9

By the twenty-seventh day of the second month the earth was completely dry.
Genesis 8:14

Never again will I destroy all living creatures … as long as the earth endures, seedtime and harvest, cold and heat, summer and winter, day and night will never cease.
Genesis 8:21-22

This final passage makes it certain that a universal flood has been sketched, for the promise is—never again. But local floods have been innumerable.

For thousands of years readers of the biblical verses understood them to mean that Noah's flood was universal, covering the whole earth, with water high over the highest mountains. Most first-time readers come to the same conclusion, millions of Christians in total. But it is not universally so today. *Most commentaries on Genesis that discuss the issue settle for a local flood in the Mesopotamian region* or somewhat wider to destroy humans who had not yet covered the planet. But are they correct? The chief reason for this change is the geological and archaeological evidence that there never was a global flood. That should not influence any plain teaching of Scripture.

The issue is very important because it affects the conclusions we draw about the nature and origin of the fossilized creatures in the earth beneath our feet all over the present world. Our belief in this matter will determine other beliefs such as the nature of the geologic column and the age of the earth. It will also influence our attitude to modern science and its teachings. Most important of all it could change our approach to the interpretation of the Bible.

The problem concerns interpretation of the Bible, not its inspiration. *And while the Bible is infallible in all it intends to teach, the same cannot be said of its interpreters.* Most Christians believe there was a Noah and a flood, and that God punished the wicked and delivered the righteous man Noah and his family. A minority view the story as only an inspired parable without any historical basis.

While the language of the event clearly describes a universal flood many objections have been raised to that understanding. The Bible frequently uses hyperbolic language such as when we are told in the Gospels that all the world was taxed in the days of Tiberius Caesar. Another objection is that the amount of water required by a universal deluge would be eight times more than the world now contains. And where did all those floodwaters subside to?

A very great problem concerns the Ark's cargo. How would the many thousands of species from all over the world get to Noah? How would huge land creatures cross the oceans? Could a mere eight people care for all these passengers? How much food would have been needed for so many? Could Noah have been a "preacher of righteousness" to the Aborigines in Australia and the inhabitants of the Americas, or even the ancient Near East where perhaps the oldest civilizations existed?

In Vawter's *A Path Through Genesis* we read:

> That enough water should have been created out of nothing to cover the highest mountains of the earth, that Noe should have been able to gather together specimens of the mere 519,000 distinct species of living creatures and feed and house them in an ark of whatever dimensions, would have required a series of unheard-of miracles.
> page 88

Ramm says some things that are similar: See pages 246-247, 243 of *The Christian View of Science and Scripture.*

The chief objection referred to by Ramm, however, is not always mentioned. Most Christian geologists agree with all others of their profession that there is no evidence whatever in the strata of the world that there has ever been a universal flood. Davis Young, the son of a well-known and respected conservative Biblical scholar, probably wrote the best book on the topic. This book, *The Biblical Flood*, is thorough, careful, and, according to most Christian geologists, reliable. We quote it:

By the early 1840s, a detailed geological time scale had been worked out on the basis of successions of superposed sedimentary strata distinguished by characteristic fossils. The primitive, transition, secondary, and tertiary gave way to the Precambrian, Cambrian, Silurian, Devonian, Carboniferous, Permian, Triassic, Jurassic, Cretaceous, Tertiary, and Quarternary, and the Tertiary was subdivided into Eocene, Miocene, and Pliocene strata. These rock sequences could be traced all across Europe and were always found to occupy the same relative order. Although strata of a given system might be missing locally, rocks were never found out of sequence where the strata were clearly in a right-side-up position. Rocks containing Triassic fossils were always found lower than rocks containing Jurassic fossils, for example, and rocks containing Silurian fossils were always found lower than rocks containing Devonian fossils.
pages 121-122

An obvious response arises in many minds. Why would an ark of such proportions be necessary if the flood was merely local? Why not just migrate? Youngblood gives a typical answer on page 112 of his commentary. He says that Noah's migration would not have been as strong a warning as the building of the ark. But is that answer good enough? Does the Bible record teach that, or does it present the ark as vital for the preservation of survivors?

The most well known book supporting the universal flood concept is Whitcomb and Morris's *The Genesis Flood*. These are two respected, well-educated Christian leaders. In pages 36 to 88 the authors do their best to refute the objections to their interpretation of a universal flood. Some of their argumentation commends itself to most readers. But their geology leaves everything to be desired.

It may be of interest to know the historical background of the present controversy. In the centuries up to the days of Wesley and Whitefield, the universality of the flood was taken for granted (see the old classic commentaries such as Matthew Henry, Adam Clarke, Scott, and Barnes, etc.). But geology began at the end of Wesley's century and was soon developed all over the world.

Christians in the United States in the nineteenth century had inherited the views of such men as William Buckland (1784-1856). He had originally taught that most of the fossils of earth owed their origin to the great Flood. One of those Christians was the greatest woman writer of all time—greatest in the sense of the extent of her writings—Ellen Gould White. She inherited the views of the preceding centuries about the Flood and incorporated them in her writings, especially in *Patriarchs and Prophets*.

George McCready Price took White very seriously. He was not only devout and intelligent, but also an excellent writer (though a poor geologist). I remember corresponding with him in the 1950s. He wrote several books on evolution and geology, and his views were widely disseminated. This was especially so in the United States, but I remember reading them in Australia in the 1940s. Ultimately, millions would be influenced by Price's writings. Whitcomb and Morris were two who had absorbed Price's teachings—hence their significant work *The Genesis Flood*. These devout and intelligent men wrote this book at the beginning of the 1960s, but it has not survived critical investigation.

So the problem before us is this: the Bible clearly teaches a universal flood, but neither geology nor archaeology support that teaching. The record is inspired. It comes from God. But have we interpreted it properly?

Chapter Nine Summary:

There was a great Flood, an ark, and a Noah. But whether that flood was universal or local has divided Bible interpreters. Neither geology nor archaeology testify to a universal flood millennia ago, but the Bible account definitely uses a parable about a *universal* flood. It purposely portrays the events in the life of Noah so as to replay the Creation story with Noah as the new Adam, the new head of the race. In doing so it skews "history" the way we typically understand it.

The key to the puzzle is found in Genesis 1, which pictures the creation of the universe in six days, with the sun, moon, and stars only arriving on the fourth day. Yet Job 38 says the stars existed before the world began. God is not concerned with teaching us the precise details of either science or history, but He is concerned with telling us about meaning, redemption and how to live by the gospel. We are his children.

Parables use everyday language with which we are familiar to teach abstract truth which is outside our experience. It is not wise to press every detail of a parable for historic or scientific "truth."

CHAPTER 10

Was Noah's flood universal?

Part Two: The exegetical problems
and light from God's other book

THE MOST THOROUGH scientific rebuttal of *The Genesis Flood* came from a Dutch scientist of renown. We quote him at length for two reasons. One, Dr. J. R. Van De Fliert sums up the objections since 1961 to the claims of Whitcomb and Morris by Christian geologists all over the world. See his rebuttal on the Internet, or in my larger book.

But, despite the rebuttals by geologists, we still think most readers would give the palm to Whitcomb and Morris about the argument of universal versus local (an argument based on a very literal reading of the text rather than a serious reading). J. David Pleins, in his *When the Great Abyss Opened*, recognized that the obvious intent of Genesis was to present a flood of universal proportions. In one place he comments, "It is hardly necessary to build a boat to save the entire world when everyone could just walk a few miles to escape the peril" (page 65). But if we follow Whitcomb and Morris we deny the evidence of the earth and the evidence of geology. How then can these differing viewpoints be reconciled with Scripture if at all? The following chapters will venture an answer to this vital question.

The inspired writer has purposely so presented the Flood as to make it the de-creation of the earth, and he makes Noah a second Adam for the new world. There is no intention to teach about geological matters. Genesis 6-8 tells of a real flood and a real ark, but all is couched in a parabolic setting.

God has given us the vital clue in the way he inspired the very first chapter of Genesis.[1] There the *universe* is said to have originated in six days. There is absolutely no dodging the evidence of Genesis 1:1; 2:1; 1:14-19. The Bible could not be clearer than when it states that the stars were made on the fourth day, and that our planet preceded the rest of the solar system and universe and that all the host of heaven and earth were completed by the end of the sixth day. God condescended to speak to his ancient people in terms that they knew. He was not out to teach them geology or astronomy. He could have told them about DNA, galaxies, dark matter, dark energy, and supernovae. That would have confused the readers altogether. Genesis is a theological book, not a scientific one. So understood, we can comprehend that the picture of universal devastation conveyed in chapters 6-8 tells the truth regarding the penalty for sin. The questions we have were never in the mind of the inspired writer. Let us learn theology from Scripture and science from nature. When in doubt as to what to learn from a passage in Genesis always ask, "What is the theological truth to be found here? That is for me."

And remember to thank God for his other book. The Belgic Confession says about creation that it is "a most elegant book." It is indeed. We neglect it at our peril.

---

1   The first chapter of the New Testament as well as the Old offers us a key for correct hermeneutics. The genealogy that begins the Gospel of Matthew is an inspired, artificial construct, drawn from history, but not pure history. Purposely, Matthew omits at least eight links in the genealogical chain. See the parallel genealogy in the early chapters of 1 Chronicles. Matthew also lists David twice in order to arrive finally at 6 x 7 = 42 ancestors of our Lord—a deeply symbolic number like the 70 x 7 ancestors in Luke 3 and the many sevens of Genesis 1–11.

    We have the same adjusting of history for the purpose of theology in the genealogies of Genesis chapters 10 and 46. The omniscient Father of us all knows we are more in need of spiritual truth than historical or scientific truth. Jesus frequently followed this same pedagogical approach.

CHAPTER TEN SUMMARY:

Christians in the first world are divided between "young-earthers" and "old-earthers"—that is between those who insist that the world (and some say the universe) is only a few thousand years old and those who accept the testimony of science (and its over fifty methods of measuring earth's age) that our world is very, very, old. Whitcomb and Morris's famous book, *The Genesis Flood*, has led to the creation of about 100 centres scattered over the world teaching a young earth and a universal flood. But no geologist or archaeologist respected by their peers agrees.

The riddle is solved when we understand God's purpose in Scripture is not to make us scientists or historians but to save us, and therefore there are parabolic elements in the Genesis stories of chapters 1-11. When we remember that one-third of Christ's teachings were in parabolic form as well as his many metaphorical pronouncements—"if your eye offend you, pluck it out"; "if your right hand offend thee, cut it off"; "they strain out gnats and swallow camels"; "say to this mountain, go throw yourself into the sea and it will be done"—it is not hard to recognize parabolic elements in Genesis that also come from Christ. Note, Genesis does concern a week, but it's a parabolic not a literal week.

CHAPTER 11

How old is the earth?

Part one: The evidence

THE BIBLE CANNOT rightly be used to establish even an approximate date for the age of the earth. It is nowhere interested in that topic. *When genealogies are used, the years are never totalled, and there are many omissions,* as anyone can prove by comparing Matthew 1 with the chronology of 1 Chronicles. "Begat" and "fathered" do not have in Scripture the precise meaning we give them. The terms are often applied to ancestors.[1] Archbishop Ussher was a fine Christian and an excellent scholar, but when he fixed upon 4004 B.C. for the birth of the world he made the biggest mistake of his life.

Today, there are about fifty methods for calculating the earth's age, and these yield results that approximate each other. That the world is about four and a half billion years old is now an axiom for scientists. Most of the evidence is drawn from the geologic column, astronomy, continental drift and plate tectonics, radiometric, radiocarbon, and amino acid dating.

The evidence for the great age of the earth is overwhelming and fully valid for all who really want to know. Chapters six and seven of Alan Hayward's *Creation and Evolution* summarize some of the evidence. Here is a portion from those chapters:

> For a quick mental picture of the earth's continents, think of a coating of (mostly) sedimentary rocks about a mile thick, sitting

---

1   Regarding "son of," "begat," and "fathered," the terms are often used to mean "was a descendant of" (even distant descendant) and "was an ancestor of" (even distant ancestor).

on top of what geologists call the 'basement' of igneous rock. But that one-mile thickness is only an average. The actual thickness varies enormously. In a few places the sedimentary coating has been scoured away completely, to expose the basement; in many places it is much less than a mile, and in other places it is a great deal more.

The greatest thicknesses occur near the mouths of large rivers. For instance, in regions around the delta of the Mississippi, geologists working for oil companies have measured the thickness of the sedimentary covering as more than seven miles. ... It is rather obvious that this enormous stack of sediment could not possibly have been laid down by the Mississippi in a few thousand years. This becomes even more certain when we take into account the way the river mouth has moved around during geologic time, over a distance of many hundreds of miles, leaving thick deposits wherever it has been. Clearly, millions of years must have been needed for that amount of deposition. ...

We know now that formerly the oilfields of Alberta, Texas and the great Lakes area were all beneath the sea. There was a period when thousands of feet of sedimentary rock were deposited there, and the fossils these rocks contain bear witness to their marine origin. Then a number of coral reefs grew on top of these sedimentary deposits, and these reefs eventually became fossilized into limestone. ...

Some of these reefs are massive, being about a thousand feet thick and many miles long, and must have taken many thousands of years to grow. ...

The Bahama Banks are made of limestone and a modified limestone known as dolomite, right down to the foot of the deepest borehole, which penetrated nearly 18,000 feet. ... Estimates vary of how long these enormous Banks took to grow. But all run into millions of years, since it is inconceivable that they could have grown in a short period of time. The present rate of growth, which is not necessarily the same as past rates of growth, is about one inch in a hundred years. ...

The Green River shale deposits in Wyoming, Utah, and Colorado ... there are up to several million successive bands. (It usually takes two layers to make one annual growth band, or varve.) ...

There are seventeen radioactive nuclides with half-lives above 80 million years—and *every one* of them does occur naturally. This is exactly what we would expect if they and the solar system are about four or five billion years old. ... The odds against this distribution 'just happening' to occur by pure chance ... are worse than a million billion to one. This means that the distribution of the radioactive nuclides provides a positively overwhelming argument for an ancient earth.
pages 88-89, 91, 92, 93, and 111.

Yellowstone National Park has forty-four successive forests petrified one upon another. Volcanic ash repeatedly has gradually weathered into soil for the next layer. R. M. Ritland and S. L. Ritland wrote a fascinating article on this topic. It is entitled *The Fossil Forests of the Yellowstone Region,* and it is found in the journal *Spectrum,* 1974, (Issues 1 and 2), pages 19-65. Its evidence for the age of the earth is quite incontrovertible.

The evidence for an ancient earth is overwhelming. In a recent article, Ritchie Way has collated and condensed many scientific findings. Portions of his article are cited:

Geochronologists have at least eleven different methods of radiometric dating at their disposal. Three of these methods have been used to date minerals from an ancient volcanic ash-bed in southern Saskatchewan, Canada. The potassium/argon method revealed their age to be 72.5 million years, plus or minus a small percentage. The uranium/lead method dated the ash at 72.4 million years plus or minus a bit. And the rubidium/strontium method said the ash was 72.54 million years old, plus or minus a little. The date determined by one method is thus corroborated or contradicted by other methods.

There are inconsistencies in determining dates, especially in the dating of lava from recent eruptions, but these are rare inconsistencies in a vast catalogue of consistencies where there is an amazing correlation of dates between the different isotopic methods. The causes of inconsistencies are being studied, and the time will come when they will be understood and accounted for. ...

Vast chalk beds occur over large areas of Northern Europe. Those in southern England are about 405 metres thick. The well-known White Cliffs of Dover are chalk. In fact, if all the chalk in the world were spread out evenly, it would cover the whole planet to a depth of 450 millimetres. ...

Chalk is a soft rock that consists mainly of coccoliths, the microscopic shells of marine organisms, and foraminifera (forams for short). Warm tropical seas dissolve atmospheric carbon dioxide (CO_2), which cocolithophores and foraminifera use to create their shells. When the coccolithophores and foraminifera die their microscopic calcium carbonate shells sink to the bottom to form a layer of chalk.

These chalk beds were laid down over a period of thirty to thirty-five million years during the Late Cretaceous period. *It has been estimated that it took one thousand years to lay down fifteen millimetres of chalk.* The computation is based on the thickness of the chalk and the time it took to deposit it, as calculated by isotopic dates of chalk from the top and bottom of the layer. Consider, on the basis of this estimate, how long it would have taken to lay down 400 metres.

The purity of the chalk beds testifies that they were laid down in calm water. Had they been laid down during the Flood—which young-earth Creationists claim was so turbulent it created the sedimentary layers of the geologic column—the chalk would have either not formed, or would have been contaminated with a great deal of sediment.
Ritchie Way, *Good News for Adventists*, September 2010

Here in this chapter we have linked the evidence from life forms (as in chalk) with the evidence for an abiotic Earth. This rightly assumes that it was not long after the cooling of the planet that minute life forms began.

Consider this from Michael W. Holm:

> Fundamentalists may attack one dating method or another, pointing out sources of error and uncertainty. But this is like walking into a forest and denying its existence because many of the trees have imperfections. The present system of geochronology is too coherent to be overthrown by attacking two or three or five or ten of the techniques employed.
> "Some persistent problems of geochronology," *Claremont Dialogue,* 2:30

Even the very conservative Seventh-day Adventist denomination now has scientists who acknowledge that the universe is 13.6 billions years old, and that this earth is 4.5 billion years old. That is progress indeed![2]

(It is important to know that when Christian and non-Christian writers speak in a derogatory way about "Creationists" almost always they are referring to those who hold to a very young earth—up to 10,000 years, and the belief that the geologic column is the result of a universal flood in Noah's day. There are millions of earnest Christians who cherish these two beliefs. Of course, they are very precious to God, and it is with some pain that I record criticisms of them despite the fact that the criticisms are correct. The traditional errors must be challenged otherwise there will be a continuing loss of young people from organized religion after university conditioning.)

2   B. Manners, "A Scientist on Creation," *Record,* 11 March 1995, pages 6-9; M. deGroot, "God and the Big Bang," *Record,* 24 October 1992, pages 6-8.

Chapter Eleven Summary:

"Young-earthers," beloved of God, may yet be in error. They forget or do not know that the Bible chronologies have gaps in them. Matthew in chapter one omits at least eight generations, and terms like "father," "son," and "begat" have different meanings to those we now assign. Father can mean ancestor, and son can mean descendant. There are many gaps in Bible history, because mere history is not primary in God's purpose. Even the Gospels omit almost all of the first thirty years of Christ's life (about ninety percent).

Thousands of Christian geologists began their careers believing in a 6,000-year-old earth, but they are now aware that the earth is actually four-and-a-half billion years old. The evidence chiefly comes from geology, astronomy, continental drift and plate tectonics, and radiometric dating and amino acid dating. Thousands of oil wells are drilled on the basis of geological information about the sedimentary layers of earth beneath our feet.

There are river varves that tell the same story as tree rings. In one well known area—the Green River shale deposits of Wyoming, Utah, and Colorado—there are up to several million successive bands. Ice-cores tell the same story. Yellowstone National Forest has 44 successive forests petrified one upon another. Volcanic ash repeatedly has weathered into soil for the next layer. Chalk beds, which can be over 400 metres thick, are composed of minute fossils that took ages to form into such places as the White Cliffs of Dover.

Unless we rightly inform our youth they will give up the Christian faith when they learn the real facts about earth's age from their teachers at University.

CHAPTER 12

How old is the earth?

Part two: Suffering, the Geologic Column, and the Cross

MANY CHRISTIANS HAVE great reservations about the geologic column because the very thought of constant suffering and death over millions of years is anathema. Several things need to be said here. *First the nineteenth-century belief in a world "red in tooth and claw" has come under critical survey and rejection.* Even Darwin's idea that competition led to the extinction of most living creatures is now rejected. Then we have to ask ourselves even about our world of today—if life were never taken by other life would the world be liveable? Would not the air be filled so with birds that we could hardly move and the sea glutted with fish and the earth crammed to overflowing? The inevitable result would be mass starvation. There had to be a way to solve the problem of fertility's dangers. Which is best—for animals to die of sickness very gradually with old age, or to have life mainly taken away quickly? But there is more yet.

The first chapters of Genesis tell us that vegetable matter and fruit were for the food of human and animals. This, of course, meant "death" for the items eaten. Many Christians quote Romans 5:12 to prove that death only came after the Fall. *But the passage is talking about human death.*

C. S. Lewis speaks very wisely:

> It is impossible at this point not to remember a certain sacred story which, though never included in the creeds, has been widely believed in the Church and seems to be implied in

several Dominical, Pauline, and Johannine utterances—I mean the story that man was not the first creature to rebel against the Creator, but that some older and mightier being long since became apostate and is now the emperor of darkness and (significantly) the Lord of this world. ... It seems to me, therefore, a reasonable supposition, that some mighty created power had already been at work for ill on the material universe, or the solar system, or, at least, the planet earth, before ever man came on the scene; and that when man fell, someone had indeed, tempted him. ... If there is such a person, as I myself believe, it may well have corrupted the animal creation before man appeared. *The Problem of Pain*, pages 193-195

Charles Spurgeon believed that *the Fall cast its shadow backwards.* This should not surprise us when we read in the New Testament that Christ was slain from the foundation of the world. Time for God is not the same as time for us. The Bible distinguishes between *kairos* time and *chronos* time. The former usually alludes to some high point in God's plan, whereas the second only has to do with the duration of days and months and years as we know it. The question has often been asked, "Do prayers after the event have any possible bearing on results?" C. S. Lewis with good reason answered "Yes," because God has foreseen our prayers. We must not bind God up with the chains that the calendar and clock put upon us. We know that the Cross casts its glorious shadow backwards as well as forwards. All the saints of the Old Testament are to be saved because of the Calvary event. Similarly the Fall *casts its shadow backwards*, and this when joined with the activity of the great adversary (mentioned earlier) should explain for us the problem about suffering and death before the arrival of *Homo sapiens*.

Why do we protest so vigorously about things beyond our knowledge and for which we have no answer? Are there not a million mysteries in our immediate environment for which we have no solution? Christ says, "What is that to thee? Follow thou me." Remember he who held the stars in his hands gave up independent power and suffered infinitely (for he was an infinite being). The Cross looked like pain, waste, and despair—all those things that sicken us as we think of the past ages before man appeared. But the fruit of Calvary's horror is glory and a safeguarding of the universe forever and ever. Paul wrote that we in this world are a theatre to the *cosmos*—the universe. See 1 Corinthians 4:9. Experimentation with sin by free-willed creatures will leave such a scar (the wounds of the Son of God) that never again will any rebel throughout eternity.

May I quote two strange bedfellows—Charles Darwin and C. S. Lewis? Their words are worthy of being written in gold and to ponder them will lift to a great degree the concern we have over the sufferings of both past and present, of animals and humans. First Darwin, in the *Origin*, page 72 of the Oxford University Press reprint of the second edition. The last lines of chapter 3: *"The war of nature is not incessant, … no fear is felt … death is generally prompt."*

Now C.S. Lewis. Read it very slowly and meditate upon it (*The Problem of Pain*, pages 103-104):

> *The Christian doctrine of suffering explains, I believe, a very curious fact about the world we live in.* The settled happiness and security which we all desire, God withholds from us by the very nature of the world: but joy, pleasure, and merriment, He has scattered broadcast. We are never safe, but we have plenty of fun, and some ecstasy. It is not hard to see why. The security we crave would teach us to rest our hearts in this world and oppose an obstacle to our return to God: a few moment of happy love, a landscape, a symphony, a merry meeting with our friends, a battle or a football match, have no such tendency. Our Father refreshes us on the journey with some pleasant inns, but will not encourage us to mistake them for home.

We must never make the problem of pain worse than it is by vague talk about the 'unimaginable sum of human misery'. Suppose I have a toothache of intensity x: and suppose that you, who are seated beside me, also begins to have a toothache of intensity x. You may, if you choose, say that the total amount of pain in the room is now 2x. But you must remember that no one is suffering 2x: search all time and all space and you will not find that composite pain in anyone's consciousness. There is no such thing as a sum of suffering, for no one suffers it. *When we have reached the maximum that a single person can suffer, we have, no doubt, reached something very horrible, but we have reached all the suffering there ever can be in the universe. The addition of a million fellow sufferers adds no more pain.*

CHAPTER TWELVE SUMMARY:

We cringe when we think of the record of death in the geologic column. But it is vital to remember, as C. S. Lewis, has pointed out, that there is a powerful enemy of God, Satan, who undoubtedly did all he could to bring suffering and death amidst God's original creation.

If animals did not die their multiplication would so fill the seas that we could walk over the waters as on land, and the air would be difficult to breathe because filled with birds. Obviously the elephants in Eden took life as they trod the virgin forests and when our first parents ate fruit they took life. When Romans 5 talks of death and sin, it is the sin of the first man that is in focus not animal death.

Besides C.S. Lewis's *The Problem of Pain* most readers would appreciate chapter 20 of *God in the Dock*. Here is one of his quotations in that chapter from pages 169-170:

> Even the severest injuries in most invertebrate animals are almost if not quite painless in the view of most biologists. Loeb collected much evidence to show that animals without cerebral hemispheres are indistinguishable from plants in every psychological respect.

How old is the earth?

Part three: Ussher's Chronology, the age of the Earth, the date of the Flood, the date of the Tower of Babel, and the six days of Genesis chapter 1

NOWHERE DOES THE Bible suggest the date of Creation, or the Flood, or the Tower of Babel. But for over 400 years most Christians have accepted dates often found in old editions of the King James' version, beginning with 4004 B.C., in the margin of Genesis chapter 1, 2348 B.C. in the margin of Genesis 9, and 2218 B.C. for the Tower of Babel in the margin of Genesis 11.

Today, no Bible chronologist in the whole world accepted by his peers agrees with these dates. They originated at the beginning of the eighteenth century and were taken for granted by many Christians for four centuries. We have the learned Archbishop James Ussher to thank (or condemn) for these dates. Nowadays, it is generally agreed that it is not possible to date from Scripture any event before the call of Abraham about 1921 B.C.

By the twentieth century, historians knew much about the early cultures of Europe, Babylonia, and other contemporary cultures. Even very conservative *Bible Dictionaries* such as that published by the Seventh-day Adventist Church depart from Ussher. On page 291 of this volume we read: "The beginning of Egyptian history with the first dynasty ... is now dated by Egyptologists between 3100 B.C. and 2800 B.C."

Ussher had approximately 250 years between the dispersion after

Babel and the call of Abraham, but it is quite impossible to put the birth of empires and cultures into that tiny slot. Writing began with the Sumerians and other cultures about 3000 B.C. There are other national groups, including the Akkadian and the Canaanite, which long precede Ussher's date for the Flood.

At the time of the call of Abraham, Ur's civilization was already growing old after many centuries of cultural supremacy. It must be remembered that it takes centuries for a high culture to develop from original small families. The whole history of the ancient Near East denies the dates of Ussher. There were several different races and cultures flourishing at least seven hundred years before Ussher's date for the Flood, and different languages approximately 1,000 years before the Tower of Babel.

Ussher failed to recognize what all chronologists now believe, that *the Bible chronologies were never meant to be timelines.* They frequently have omissions as in the first chapter of the New Testament. The terms "father," "son," and "begat," had far wider meaning in Bible times than recognized by Ussher's very literalistic reading of Scripture. The chronologies give us high points of sacred history. The greatest mistake made by those who wish to literalize the time indications of Genesis is that it misses the meaning of the Bible's first verse. To all Jewish scholars of note it reads: "In the beginning God created the universe." This verse comprehends all that follows in the chapter, just as Genesis 2:1 comprehends all that had happened in that same opening chapter. The evidence for this is manifold but includes the fact that *"heaven and earth" throughout the Scriptures signifies the Universe.* Earth is our planet, and "heavens" signifies all the rest of the Universe. In Genesis 1:14-18 we are told of the creation of the sun, moon, and stars, that is, the majority of the Universe mentioned in verse 1. The Hebrew word here for "made" is the typical one used elsewhere and never means "appeared" as some would prefer.

In view of these facts it is clear that the six days of Genesis 1 constitute a parabolic week for all the time involved in God's origination of the entire universe. God has stooped to use the analogy of the human working week. Thus the record particularly means to stress the importance of the first religious institution, the Sabbath.

It has been suggested that this present book should offer precise dates for earth's beginning, the arrival of Adam and Eve and the Fall, and for the culture and events of Genesis chapters 4, 9, and 11. No one on earth can do that. We do know that the universe is about 14 billion years old, and that this planet (beyond all legitimate controversy) is about 4.5 billion years old. Adam and Eve were God's climactic creations after the progressive arrival of all preceding life forms. The date of their arrival nobody knows. Many Christian scientists believe it must been somewhere between 200,000 B.C. and 100,000 B.C. The Fall probably happened soon after, but then there is a great gap after the pristine chapters two and three of Genesis which have no hint of other mortals, domesticity of animals, cities, and high culture. Adam is not used as a proper name in Genesis 1-3 as the Hebrew used proves and as appears in practically all modern translations, but the word does appear as a proper name in Genesis 4 onwards. After chapter 11 it drops out again. There are other names in the initial record of Genesis that also have a different meaning when used later, if used at all.

There is practically no scholarly controversy concerning the existence of a paleolithic world prior to about 10,000 B.C. and the Neolithic world that followed. Genesis 4 fits the latter with its mention of cities, domesticity of plants and animals, and various forms of culture. *These distinguish chapter 4 from the preceding three chapters.* All of this that great man Archbishop James Ussher—an outstanding scholar for his times—would have happily accepted had he known what it is possible for modern bishops and their congregations to now know.

CHAPTER THIRTEEN SUMMARY:

Archbishop Ussher's chronology found in the margins of many KJV Bibles is based on erroneous premises and is no longer accepted by Bible chronologists.

Precise dates for events before Abraham are unknown.

The mysteries of Genesis 1-11

Part one: Chapters 1-11 are a different genre to chapters 12-50

WE RETURN NOW to the most controversial and most closely studied chapters in the Bible. Unbelief in these is the excuse offered by many for their rejection of Christ. Christians must wrestle with the problems implicit here and do it very prayerfully.

Most scholars see Genesis 1-11 as a different genre to chapters 12-50. It covers an unknown vista of time whereas chapters 12-50 encompass only about five centuries. Genesis 1-11 is a global introduction to the history of one localized unknown tribe. And it begins with the Creation of the universe—about 14 billion years ago. Anyone who reads both sets will see the difference immediately. Everything here in the early chapters is "gigantesque." It is mega-history—that is, very great history. We have no analogies from everyday life to the unique events of these pages. We have never seen the creation of a universe. The Hebrew word for "created" always has God as its subject; it refers to a supernatural work that none of us has ever seen.

Nor have we encountered a paradise with abundant waters, gold and gems, and trees of life and the knowledge of good and evil. We have never met a walking snake who can talk, or people who have lived to the ages offered us in the genealogies of chapters 5 and 11. We have not met giants like those of Genesis 6:4, or so mighty a hunter as Nimrod, and certainly not wicked angels who have taken human form in order to mate with earth's beautiful women (if the most popular interpretation is true). See Genesis 6:2,4. And the Flood is no ordinary flood. The account is undeniably about a universal flood.

(Note God's promise that such would never be repeated. But local floods have been common.) It covers all the highest mountains of earth to a height of about forty centimeters. You may have seen the Queen Mary or the Queen Elizabeth, but in some respects they pale alongside Noah's boat.

Most of all we have never known an omnipotent God, who is an omnipresent Spirit, to use vocal cords and condescend to the activities of a surgeon, a gardener, a walker, and a seamstress. But all these are to be found in Genesis chapters 1-3. God is a spirit according to John 4:24. The second commandment implies that. Therefore he has no vocal cords or physical parts such as we know—hands, feet, buttocks, etc.

The well-known and respected *International Commentary* edited by F. F. Bruce begins its comments on Genesis by listing the immediate problems confronting every exegete. These include the apparent clash between science and Genesis 1, the size of Noah's Flood, the antiquity of man, and the chronology (human ages) of chapters 5 and 11. Most modern commentaries do the same unless they choose to avoid the problems in their exegesis (which many do). No wonder that this is the most intensely studied portion of the whole Bible and to many Christians the most difficult. So, let's get into it.

As the inspired prologue of Scripture and the foundation of the rest of the Bible, *these chapters have several layers of meaning not always apparent at first view.* The corrupting and ever spreading impact of sin is its chief theme, and the false views of God, the world, and man are here corrected. The Cross is here, as is the everlasting gospel. It is a "tract for the times" and a tract for all time. *As with the parabolic teaching of Jesus (one-third of the whole of his recorded words) there are depths beyond the surface.* This is what we would expect from the Spirit of Christ who inspired both Testaments. The people we meet from Adam to Noah are real people. We will read of actual events like Creation, the Fall, and the Flood, but the accounts are put in semi-parabolic settings that more may be taught us than a prosaic history could.

These chapters are about sin and salvation, judgment and redemption, and the privileges and responsibilities of worship. But they are also related to the problems threatening the earliest people of God, and pagan errors are subtly rebutted. Like every part of Scripture this too had to make sense to those who first heard or read it. It was not just written for the twenty-first century. If we are to understand its depths we must become acquainted with the mental and physical milieu of ancient Mesopotamia, from whence Abraham came, and Egypt, from which Moses came. And chapters 2 to 11 find their key in chapter 1.

Even secular writers have understood the literary nature of Genesis one. Consider the following from a secular work entitled, *Evolution the Great Debate*, written by Vernon Blackmore and Andrew Page and published in 1989:

> We may toy with many 'creation stories' to satisfy our longings but Genesis wants to put the record straight. We were created by God.
>
> With this in mind the early chapters of Genesis may be seen as an antidote to false faith rather than as a lesson in biological origins. Within the structure of the Bible's first chapter there is much to suggest a stylistic form ... the possibility of a literary rather than a scientific structure. We must find the clues within the text. And here we can note a parallelism between the first three days of creation and the last three days. In days one to three, God creates the light, the sky and water, and then the earth. In days four to six he makes occupants for these realms of creation: the stars, [sun and moon], the birds and fishes, the animals and people. The message is not scientific, but theological. The author is tracing out the totality of creation. We owe our being to God. The whole world is his, with nothing outside his power.
>
> The author [is] using the thought forms of his day to express deeper (and older) revealed truths about God. Where the Babylonians believed in many gods, Genesis stresses that God is one. Where the Babylonians sought to appease their rather capricious deities, Genesis upholds God as benevolent and providential. ... What better instrument to instruct the young, brought up in a culture riddled with false beliefs in many gods?
> pages 130-131

Henry Drummond, beloved author of the *The Greatest Thing in the World,* was a theistic evolutionist. We disagree with him there, but acknowledge the truthfulness of the following lines from his pen with reference to Genesis chapter one:

> There was no science then. Scientific questions were not even asked then. To have given men science would not only have been an anachronism, but a source of mystification and confusion all along the line. The almost painful silence—indeed, the absolute sterility—of the Bible with regard to science is so marked as to have led men to question the very beneficence of God. Why was not the use of the stars explained to navigators, or chloroform to surgeons? Why is a man left to die on the hillside when the medicinal plant which would save him, did he but know it, lies at his feet? What is it to early man to know how the moon was made? What he wants to know is how bread is made. How fish are to be caught, fowls snared, beasts trapped and their skins tanned—these are his problems. Doubtless there are valid reasons why the Bible does not contain a technological dictionary and a pharmacopoeia, or anticipate the *Encyclopaedia Britannica.* But that it does not inform us on these practical matters is surely a valid argument why we should not expect it to instruct the world in geology. ...

> Genesis is a presentation of one or two great elementary truths to the childhood of the world. It can only be read aright in the spirit in which it was written, with its original purpose in view, and its original audience. What did it mean to them? What would they understand by it? What did they need to know and not know?

> To expand the constructive answers to these questions in detail does not fall within our province here. What we have to note is that a scientific theory of the universe formed no part of the original writer's intention. Dating from the childhood of the world, written for children, and for that child-spirit in man which remains unchanged by time, it takes colour and shape accordingly. Its object is purely religious, the point being, not how certain things were made, but that God made them. It is

not dedicated to science, but to the soul. It is a sublime theology, given in view of ignorance or idolatry or polytheism, telling the worshipful youth of the world that the heavens and the earth and every creeping and flying thing were made by God. ...

The first principle which must rule our reading of this book is the elementary canon of all literary criticism, which decides that any interpretation of a part of a book or of a literature must be controlled by the dominant purpose or *motif* of the whole. And when one investigates that dominant purpose in the case of the Bible, he finds it reducing itself to one thing—religion.
George Adam Smith, *The Life of Henry Drummond*, pages 258, 260-261, 262

As the first verse of the Bible abolishes all fashionable philosophical errors like polytheism, materialism, dualism, atheism, skepticism, etc., so now in the first institutions—Sabbath and marriage—we have further protection for humanity. Our present world is in chaos because both these appointments are now widely neglected. Any society that is careless regarding these institutions disintegrates. Those who refuse to give a day to God cannot live properly and so jeopardize eternity. "When the holy day becomes the day of man, society and humanity withers away and the demons rule." Those who abuse the family relationships have no protection against other fatal sins.

Young men who grow up without fathers are hundreds of times more likely to go to jail, and the loss of a parent for a young woman is similarly costly. In most cities young men carouse in drunkenness and violence because they do not know and acknowledge God. They are angry because they see no meaning in life. We first learn about God from the behaviour and teaching of godly parents. The blood-baths of the last century with its hundred wars, and the near break up of marriage in some countries testify to the results of neglecting the divinely appointed institutions. The family is the seed and the prophecy of society. Half a billion people have died in the approximately 14,500 wars this world has seen. Had Genesis chapters 1 and 2 been known and believed by mankind what sorrows could have been averted! When one becomes aware of the spiritual depths of the early chapters of the Bible its difficulties are superseded.

Genesis is not anti-scientific nor pre-scientific, but non-scientific. Scientific views change from generation to generation, but holiness, the reflection of God, never changes. And there can be no lasting happiness without holiness. Sin is suicide and insanity, but purity is paradise. How very practical Scripture is! History can be interpreted in many different ways, and historians differ in their opinion, but holiness is so clearly identified in the person of Jesus Christ that all unanswered questions have little weight.

CHAPTER FOURTEEN SUMMARY:

Genesis chapters 1-11 have occasioned more controversy and evoked more intense study than any other portion of Scripture. What we have here is mega-history, "gigantesque" phenomena that have much to teach us. These chapters transcend what we now know in daily experience. We have never seen a creation, an Eden, giants, people who live nearly one thousand years, and a tower aimed at reaching heaven, etc.

The people we meet in these chapters are real people, and Creation, the Fall, and the Flood were real events. But they are told us in such a way as to teach us much more than straightforward prose ever could. One picture is worth a thousand words, and we have many pictures in these inspired chapters.

It is not necessary to worry about how Noah could fit in his vessel so many thousands of genera some of which had to traverse oceans and mountains. It is, however vital, to understand that sin brings judgment and that only righteousness in Christ can save us. (Deut. 29:29).

Chapter 15

The Mysteries of Genesis 1-11

Part two: Interpretation

IT HAS NOT been sufficiently observed that Genesis 1 illustrates the condescension of God as he stoops to portray creation in terms understandable to the first recipients of Genesis thousands of years ago. The chapter offered its first readers the certainty that the universe as they knew it came from their Maker. *The statement that sun, moon, and stars were made on the fourth day is our clue to understanding the whole chapter properly, as well as the ones that follow.*[1] It seems strange to us that the planet should be made before sun, moon, and stars, but it was not at all strange to the first readers of Moses. Remember the Bible speaks about seventy-five times of the sun rising and setting, whereas in reality it does neither. It also speaks of the four corners of the earth and the four winds of heaven. All this reflects the language of cultural appearance.

The expression "heaven and earth" is a well-known merism that means "everything." Thus many modern translators translate Genesis 1:1: "In the beginning God created the universe." The universe known to the ancients consisted of earth, sun, moon and about 6,000 stars, and the earth was the center of all with the heavenly bodies revolving around it. Genesis 2:1 is referring to the stars by the term "host." So, the whole universe is comprehended as being made in six days. Similar adaptations to the first readers continue in the following chapters (particularly 6, 7, and 8) until we reach the story of Abraham.

We are endeavouring to follow the counsel of today's evangelical

---

1   Some think Genesis 1 is saying that the heavenly bodies appeared on the fourth day. The Hebrew text does not support that.

scholars about reading Genesis in the light of its original readership and their milieu. Towards the close of the nineteenth century archaeologists found on clay tablets in Mesopotamia and elsewhere stories from Israel's neighbors, which in many ways paralleled Genesis 1-11, and especially chapters 1, and 6-8. These include *Enuma Elish*, *The Atrahasis Epic* and the *Gilgamesh Epic*. The first one is a mythological account of creation, but the latter two include the great Flood of about 3000 B.C., which had indelibly inscribed a memory on Mesopotamia and other lands.

On the eleventh tablet of the *Gilgamesh Epic* is a lengthy flood story in poetic form. We can summarize the main points as follows: a great boat is built by command of the gods; it is sealed by pitch and built of specific dimensions (smaller than Noah's vessel); clean and unclean animals are taken aboard. The hero and a few others are saved, and the boat finally rests on a mountain. Both a raven and a dove are sent out; the gods soon sniff the odour of pleasing sacrifices.

But let us be more specific. There are seventeen points of congruence between the Gilgamesh story and Genesis.

It is almost universally agreed that neither writer copied from the other. The Genesis story differs in significant respects such as the divine promise in 8:21,22 and the initial sending from the ark of a dove not a raven. Nevertheless it is perfectly clear that the writer of Genesis knew the Gilgamesh story and has purposely reproduced many elements of it. We are reminded of Genesis 1 where the creation account in some ways mimics the Mesopotamian myth of *Enuma Elish*, but carefully avoids its polytheism and immorality.

The inspired writer of Genesis was led to use well-known stories to make significant points and rebut pagan errors at the same time. A well-known evangelical scholar, G. J. Wenham, wrote an article on Genesis 6-8 called "The Coherence of the Flood Narrative," in *Vetus Testamentum*, Volume 28, 1978, pages 336-348. Wenham points out that the Genesis story is a theological one. For example, as with Creation in Genesis 1, the Flood begins on Sunday and ends on Friday. Noah apparently was a Sabbath-keeper. As with Genesis one, the chapters on Noah's flood diverge from the pagan stories at key theological points. Monotheism prevails, and the crudities and licentiousness of pagan gods are shunned. Key extras are found as mentioned above. The God of Genesis and of Noah's Flood has a tender heart despite his impeccable concern for holiness (see 8:21-22). No pagan society ever had a true Sabbath, but that institution is prominent in Genesis. Its establishment proves that the Genesis stories are not dependent on the pagan accounts, but they transform them.

As surely as the Lord of glory humbled himself by birth in a cowshed, and by using the speech of a little-known people, even telling them stories, so his Spirit led Moses to teach those under his care by histories, and parables and pictures that they could understand all that was necessary despite their abysmal ignorance.

Chapter Fifteen Summary

All of Scripture had meaning for its first recipients and it is important to understand that Genesis was originally written for believers surrounded by idolaters with dangerous and erroneous beliefs. Genesis alludes repeatedly to well-known ancient polytheistic traditions and rescues what has value, transforming the same. The Flood story has seventeen parallels to the ancient Sumerian Flood stories. Let us remember that Christ once told a story (Luke 16:19-31) based on erroneous beliefs of his day. Heaven and earth are not in shouting distance and neither does Hades (the grave) hold an ever-burning hell.

CHAPTER 16

The Mysteries of Genesis 1-11:

Part Three: Clues

BESIDES THE SUMERIAN records, there are others including Egyptian ones, and the Genesis author is subtly rebutting the erroneous religious ideas in all of these. So he protects his Israelite contemporaries (for whom Genesis was first written) from pagan errors, follies, and vices.

It must be kept in mind *that all eleven chapters reflect elements from the myths of surrounding nations.* This is even true of Genesis 3. The pagans had a story of one who sought immortality from a very special herb, and a serpent figures in that story. The genealogies of chapters 5 and 11 are reminiscent of king lists of Sumeria (one of which had ten long-lived kings before the flood, and ten after, as with Genesis). The seventh king in the Sumerian list gained immortality as did Enoch the seventh from Adam. The covenant set forth in Genesis 9 has in it the rainbow—(the union of sunshine and shower typifying God's love and justice) for its symbol. The rainbow will meet us again in the Bible's last book (Revelation chapters 4 and 10). It was a well-known symbol with the Sumerians and is found in the *Epic of Gilgamesh*. The narrative of the tower of Babel has long been recognized as reflecting the ziggurats of proud Babylon. Even the number seven which is so prominent in Genesis is also prominent in the pagan stories. When Christ wished to feed many thousands of hungry people he took what was available, a few loaves and fishes, and he transformed them to the glory of God. In inspiring some sections of Holy Scripture he has followed a similar principle.

Imagine for a moment that you were God. You wish to write a book that would make sense and give help to the first recipients as well as to countless generations thereafter. How would you do it? Suppose you wished to make it very scientific, which science would you offer? That of the third millennium before Christ, or that of our Lord's time, or the science of the Middle Ages, or of our day, or the best science which is yet to come? And if you decided to use history would it be with the purpose of making historians, or of helping people who love you to know how to live?

As our Savior was a union of the human and the divine, the Son of God, but also the Son of Man, so it is with Scripture. Scripture is not given us in the language of heaven, but the signs of ancient languages were employed by the inspiring Spirit. Scripture is not perfect in everything (even its customary published form is somewhat plain though it houses jewels within) but it is perfect for its purpose. That purpose is plainly told us in John 20:31. "These are written that you might know that Jesus is the Christ and that you might have life through his name." When Calvin wrote his *Commentary on Genesis* he told his readers to go to astronomy if they wanted details about the heavens. Neither Moses nor Christ set out to teach anything that could be found out by human effort. Read from Matthew 1:1 to John 21:25, and you will not find one jot of instruction from Christ about anything unrelated to his purpose in coming to this planet.

The intention of Scripture is based on an overarching concern for the well-being of all of us. Are we meaningless clots of coincidental molecules, or are we truly children of God? Genesis 1:26-28 answers that question. And even modern science confirms that answer. We now know that everything in the universe is for us—the sidereal heavens and their galaxies, and every living creature, as well as the basic laws of the universe. (Read Michael Denton's *Nature's Destiny* for the evidence). Shakespeare could write about "books in the running brooks and sermons in stones and good in everything." Thereby, he echoes God's intention in creation. It is not by chance that we are familiar with the lowly caterpillar which enters its chrysalis as though in death, and then emerges in resurrection as a gorgeous butterfly. God has done all that could be done to encourage us to fight the battles of life with the knowledge that we are important because we are his children, infinitely loved, and with the potential of immortality. Even death has no fears for the believer.

What do you most want to know? Pure history or how to live? Which is more important to you, the historical facts of the third millennium B.C., or the truth about God, salvation, and Judgment Day? When Christ spoke about cutting off our right hand, or plucking out our eye, turning the other cheek, camels going through the eyes of needles, and moving mountains into the sea, did he intend that we should take him literally or seriously? When he spoke about forgiving seventy times seven, did he intend that we should count up to 489 and then let fly? Why do the Gospels practically ignore the first thirty years of Christ's life? Would not that history have been fascinating?

We remember that one-third of Christ's recorded teaching was expressed in parables. Then remember that it was the Spirit of Christ who inspired the Old as well as the New Testament. There are parables in the Old Testament also. See Judges 9 and 2 Samuel 12. Many have seen the book of Job as one great poetic parable. Certainly the Song of Solomon is not what we would expect for religious prose. There are many types of literature in the Bible—poetry, prose, law, apocalyptic, proverbs, history, litany, parable, and rhetoric, etc. *Nobody takes every part of the Bible literally.* No one uses "all things are yours" (1 Cor. 3:21) as an excuse for stealing. What Christian takes literally the words "there is no God" found more than once in Psalms? Does the Christian male reader take literally the words, "If you be circumcised Christ shall profit you nothing?" Even Paul's words about women being silent in church must be read in context rather than foolishly sitting dogmatically on certain sentences alone. Who takes 1 Corinthians 7:1 literally? "Now, concerning the things whereof ye wrote unto me: It is good for a man not to touch a woman."

In Matthew 13 our Lord constantly draws from the secular world to make his points. In Matthew 22 we read of a King's marriage feast—well, that's all right, but then we read that those who were invited murdered the inviting messengers. And that just does not make sense—until we recognize that Christ was warning his own would-be murderers. Genesis 1-11 also has strange parabolic elements, but all convey eternal truth.

With these things in mind we can better understand the conclusions of great evangelical Christians who have studied the Bible more closely than most of us. *Old Testament Survey,* from scholars of Fuller Theological Seminary, is a well-known textbook. Note the following from pages 20 and 21:

> Identifying the genre of Genesis 1-11 is difficult because of its uniqueness. None of these accounts belong to the genre 'myth.' Nor is any of them 'history' in the sense of eyewitness, objective reporting. Rather they convey theological truth about events, portrayed in a largely symbolic, pictorial literary style. This is not to say that Genesis 1-11 conveys historical falsehood. That conclusion would follow only if the material claimed to contain objective descriptions. From the above discussion it is certain that such was not the intent. On the other hand, the view that the truths taught in these chapters have no objective basis is mistaken. Fundamental truths are declared: creation of all by God, special divine intervention in the origin of the first man and woman, the unity of the human race, the pristine goodness of the created world, including humanity, the entrance of sin through the disobedience of the first pair, the rampant spread of sin after this initial act of disobedience. These truths are all based on facts. Their certainty implies the reality of the facts.

Gordon Wenham in his commentary on Genesis (53) speaks similarly:

> If it is correct to view Genesis 1-11 as an inspired retelling of ancient oriental traditions about the origins of the world with a view to presenting the nature of the true God as one, omnipotent, omniscient, and good, as opposed to the fallible, capricious, weak deities who populated the rest of the ancient world; if further it is concerned to show that humanity is central in the divine plot, not an afterthought; if finally it wants to show that man's plight is the product of his own disobedience and indeed is bound to worsen without divine intervention, Genesis 1-11 is setting out a picture of the world that is at odds, both with the polytheistic optimism of ancient Mesopotamia, and the humanistic secularism of the modern world.

Though historical and scientific questions may be uppermost in our minds as we approach the text, it is doubtful whether they were in the writer's mind, and we should therefore be cautious about looking for answers to questions he was not concerned with. Genesis is primarily about God's character and his purpose for sinful mankind. Let us beware of allowing our interests to divert us from the central thrust of the book, so that we miss what the Lord, our Creator and Redeemer, is saying to us.

Chapter Sixteen Summary:

The chief clue to interpreting Genesis 1 to 11 lies at the door—the Bible's first chapter. When we read Genesis 2:1-3 we are told that by the end of the sixth day of creation all the stars of heaven, all the planets, as well as our world had been made. God did not tell the people of Moses's day about galaxies, dark matter and dark holes, supernovae, DNA, or thermonuclear forces. He told them what they needed to know about him and their own conduct in order to make their brief sojourn here a preparation for eternity.

God is like a tall man bending down to lisp to a small child. When our children enquire of us regarding how their siblings got here we do not mystify them with truths that are not suitable for them at their age. Genesis is like that. What a wonderful book that can meet the needs of the uneducated and the learned, the young and the old, and the weak and the strong!

CHAPTER 17

Creation or Darwinism?

Part one: Naturalism and Nature's Denial

LET IT BE firmly established in the mind of every enquirer that Darwinism is Naturalism.[1] Naturalism says chance is the source of all things including the solar system, life, and the brain. (Theistic evolutionists deny this, but not the original and most vociferous proponents of the theory.) Charles Darwin, Stephen Jay Gould, G. G. Simpson, Julian and Aldous Huxley, Richard Dawkins, and a hundred others could be quoted. Here are the well-known words of Simpson: "Man is the result of a purposeless and natural process that did not have him in mind." Since 1859, the magic wand behind everything has been recognized as chance. Therefore Darwin's own "horrid doubt"—that if the brain developed from the lowest organism why trust it? Here are his own words:

> With me, the horrid doubt always arises whether the convictions of man's mind, which have been developed from the mind of the lower animals, are of any value or at all trustworthy. *Life and Letters of Charles Darwin* edited by Francis Darwin, Vol. 1, page 285

Darwinism is the source of postmodernism, which claims that ideas and beliefs are never true but may be useful. If that is true then

---

1   In most discussions it is appropriate to distinguish between methodological naturalism and philosophical naturalism. The practice of the first is, of course, the aim of all great scientists. It is right in the study of science to seek the answers from science itself. Science speaks in terms of "how" and "when," not "why" or "who." It is certain, however, that the great majority of scientists today who are Darwinians are philosophical naturalists and inevitably influenced by that conviction.

postmodernism is undercut by its own theory. If it also is not true, why should we trust it? While postmodernism rejects the concept of objectivity there is one idea it treats as objective fact—Darwinism. Tolstoy was more perceptive than Darwin. He asserted that, *"God is he without whom we cannot live."* Many are living who claim not to believe in God. But straightway after that claim they go on living as though life had some sort of meaning that made their existence of value. But even then they make an eternity of nothing and nothing of eternity and are lost. *The way to test philosophical or theological theories is to ask whether they are allied to Naturalism or Supernaturalism.*

Hence it is possible to bad-mouth atheistic evolution as a form of insanity, or at the best a myth though not recognized as such. The atheist can argue volubly never stopping to think that his trust in his argumentation has no basis if atheism is true. Note the term G.I.G.O.—garbage in, garbage out. All is garbage unless the Creator is acknowledged. Darwinism from its very source, and for most adherents, is atheistic and thereby makes all life meaningless and hopeless. Despite all these hard words, we all know many wonderfully decent people who are committed to evolution. How can that be? Because of the known great age of the earth (4.5 billion years) and the accepted reality of the testimony of the geologic column (with its single-celled creatures at the lowest point, then rising with multicelled animals, till at the top *Homo sapiens*), it is understandable that many millions have come to accept the theory of organic evolution. The evidence seems so plainly for it. We think we are using our brains to decide this issue, but in truth we usually use our brains in the same way we use a window—we take them for granted and therefore miss the fact that they constitute a primary argument in the matter under discussion. Are we not moving too fast when we assent to Darwinism? Is not an unwarranted worship of chance involved in such a faith? Do any of us actually believe that everything is chance and that nothing has value (which is the logical consequent of Darwinism)?

Denton points out the miraculous nature of living things. He writes about "the remarkable specks of organized matter that have constructed every multicellular organism that ever existed." We are surrounded by miracles of nanotechnology:

On any count the average cell must utilize close to a million unique adaptive structures and processes—more than the number in a jumbo jet ... the complexity of a jumbo jet packed into a speck of dust invisible to the human eye.
Ibid., pages 212–213

Denton clearly rejects the endeavours to disprove Michael Behe's contention that the bacterial flagellum is a creature of irreducible complexity. And he adds others of a similar nature: the amniotic egg, the avian lung, and the flight feather of a bird. For none of these is there any "conceivable series of feasible intermediates" (see page 275).

The most well known biography of Darwin (by Adrian Desmond and James Moore) endorses the previous comments regarding the historical fact that Darwin's philosophy rather than his science motivated many to follow him. Here are typical expressions from this classic:

He was sad that true believers were so few. He had turned the world to evolution, and practically no one to natural selection, not even his champions.
Darwin, page 642

But his older friends were often negative. Wollaston insisted with Coleridge that Nature is a 'pestilent abstraction' and can select nothing. ... Few were grasping natural selection, which left him cursing that 'I must be a very bad explainer.' ... 'I suppose "natural selection" was a bad term,' he admitted. 'Natural Preservation might have been less anthropomorphic.' He tried it out on Lyell. But Lyell could not read his abysmal handwriting and read it as 'Natural Persecution'.
Ibid., page 492

Hooker now admitted that Darwin's evolutionary ideas 'have possessed me, without however converting me.' ... He asked whether the barnacle work had caused Darwin to modify his theories. He had expected it to make Darwin more cautious.
Ibid., p. 373

Huxley did not know the details of natural selection, but Dar-

win never missed a chance to push his pedigree approach.
Darwin, pages 458-9

Quotations from Moore and Desmond could be multiplied, but the preceding are more than enough to prove that Gillespie and Pearcey are correct in their appraisal of the historical situation surrounding Darwinism in the years following 1859. *Darwin's friends often had a political agenda and were less interested in the details of natural selection.* They were for Naturalism, and Darwin was a great aid in the promulgation of this philosophy. *The Origin of Species* won its early victories on grounds other than science and not until the Mendelian principles of heredity were promoted by neo-Darwinism did the scientific claims of Darwin come into fuller focus.

The significance of these facts for a post-modern society should stand out. Our present world is secular to the core, and with God dethroned, the only alternative, the only game in town, has to be a "science" which makes no moral demands. The Romanian playwright Eugène Ionesco succinctly summed up the problem of naturalism:

> Cut off from his religious, metaphysical, and transcendental roots, man's actions become senseless, absurd, useless.

> Albert Camus agreed: 'Up till now, man derived his coherence from his Creator. But from the moment that he consecrates his rupture with Him, he finds himself delivered over to the fleeting moment, to the passing days, and to wasted sensibility.'
> *The Rebel*, page 47

This chapter has revolved around the basic fact that thought punctures naturalism. If everything is physically caused then determinism is true, but at the same time there can be no truth and no freedom. If determinism is true we could not know it, and every argument in its support is logically defunct for even our arguments are determined. Naturalism does not account for our primary experiences—reason, memory, conscience, and beauty. Therefore, the basis of Darwinism is null and void.

If you abide in my word ... you shall know the truth, and the truth shall make you free (John 8:31-32).

Worthy of close study is the recent book by an unbeliever of considerable reputation in the scholarly world.

Thomas Nagel, *Mind and Cosmos: Why the materialist Neo-Darwinian conception of nature is almost certainly false,* Oxford, 2012.

> It is *prima facie* highly implausible that life as we know it is the result of a sequence of physical accidents together with the mechanism of natural selection.
> page 6

> With regard to evolution, the process of natural selection cannot account for the actual history without an adequate supply of visible mutations, and I believe it remains an open question whether this could have been provided in geological time merely as a result of chemical accident, without the operation of some other factors determining and restricting the form of genetic variation. It is no longer legitimate simply to imagine a sequence of gradually evolving phenotypes, as if their appearance through mutations in the DNA were unproblematic—as Richard Dawkins does for the evolution of the eyes.
> page 9

> The intelligibility of the world is no accident.
> page 17

> I have argued patiently against the prevailing form of naturalism, a reductive materialism that purports to capture life and mind through its neo-Darwinian extension.
> page 127

Chapter Seventeen Summary:

Now we come to the chief issue threatening Christians today (apart from our own sinful natures). Did we arrive on this planet as a result of mindless forces operating over eons? If so, what is it all but "the murmur of gnats amid a billion billion suns?" Was Darwin right when he wrote *On the Origin of Species,* a book that changed the world—for the worse? It was a book that triggered aggressive warfare on a scale never known before and all the evils of Social Darwinism—greed, rapacity, cruelty, and racism. These, of course, were perversions of Darwin's teachings, not his intent.

If Darwinism is true there is no God, no afterlife, no distinction between good and evil, nothing wrong with Auschwitz, or the murders in our cities. If Darwin was right we have no grounds to criticize anything for there is no objective standard. If Darwin was right there can be no real faith, hope, or love, and no reason to live or to die. All passion is without ground and as meaningless as the mental hell confronting us.

But Darwinism was first of all a philosophy of Naturalism long before it came to be thought of as a science. His earliest friends accepted it because of its philosophic teaching not because they believed in natural selection. This truth is now universally acknowledged—it is not the invention of fundamentalist Christians. Darwinism truly challenges its believers to live an impossible life. No sane man can live atheism. We all distinguish, when driving, between a child playing on the road and a drifting paper bag.

But just as Darwin had many doubts about the reliability of his own mind (considering its origin), so today a primary issue is this: if my brain is the result of thoughtless cosmic processes, why should I trust its conclusions? Is thinking only itching? We don't call a floating cloud true or false, why trust the conclusion of a chance arrival we call the brain?

The recent discovery of the Anthropic Principle (see the books by Hugh Ross and others on this topic) outlaws the doctrines of naturalism, which are all based on chance. Chance cannot create a thimble, let alone a universe.

CHAPTER 18

Creation or Darwinism?

Part two: Dissatisfaction of scientists with neo-Darwinism

"I can see no difficulty in a race of bears being rendered,
by natural selection, more and more aquatic in their structure
and habits, with larger and larger mouths, till a creature
was produced as monstrous as a whale."
Charles Darwin, *Origin of Species,* page viii

WE WILL DISCUSS the issues at stake under four headings: "The Growing Dissatisfaction with Neo-Darwinism"; "The Evidence of Paleontology"; "The Impossibility of Chance as the Source of Everything"; "The Traditional Ape-men or Hominids". Let us begin with the first. Is there evidence that many scientists have growing doubts about the evolutionary faith they once cherished? (In the pages that follow I will be citing well-known and respected leaders in science. I am not, and never could be, one of those. Therefore my reliance in what follows is upon the specialists in fields that are not mine.)

It may come as a surprise to many that *in recent years scientific criticism of neo-Darwinism has multiplied exceedingly.* To listen to a fundamentalist scientist like Richard Dawkins one would not learn this truth, but Dawkins and Daniel Dennett and some others not only pour vicious opprobrium, pejorative attacks, on those who differ from them, but seem to have minds like concrete—all mixed up and permanently set. They are so sadly different from those evolutionists who candidly admit the increasing tide of problems faced by Darwinism. See *The Neck of the Giraffe* by Francis Hitching, *Darwin*

Retried by Norman Macbeth, *The Great Evolution Mystery* by Gordon Rattray Taylor, and many others cited by William R. Bird in his *Origin of Species Revisited,* volume one.

"The evolutionary process is rife with happenstance, incredible waste, death, pain and horror." Nevertheless, if it be true, let us embrace it. Error never grows anything good. But why do we venture to talk about truth? Should Darwinism be true, there is no such thing. If all is the result of chance then that applies to the solar system, the earth and our brains. "If my mental processes are determined solely by the movement of atoms I have no reason to believe that my beliefs are true or that my brain is composed of atoms" (J. B. S. Haldane). Which means of course that atheism, the doctrine of evolution, duty, right and wrong, ought, love, hate, murder, unselfishness, reason, hope, and faith are meaningless expletives with no basis on this accidental planet.

But while men may talk of meaninglessness or atheism, no one can live it. The most dyed-in-the-wool unbeliever has values. He cannot drive over a playing child as easily as he might drive over a brown paper bag. This obstacle of the impossibility of implementing such beliefs should make any sane person skeptical of all chance philosophies and Darwinism in particular.

It is undeniable that great changes have taken place in evolutionary beliefs. The uncompromising uniformitarianism of Lyell and Darwin have given way to acknowledging the part catastrophes have played in geological history. The most well known advocate of this "neo-catastrophism" is Derek Ager who tells us that:

> The history of any one part of the earth, like the life of a soldier, consists of long periods of boredom and short periods of terror. *The Nature of the Stratigraphical Record,* page 100

But the greatest change has been encapsulated in what is known as punctuated equilibrium that plainly asserts that at least most of the Creationists' "missing links" are indeed missing. And there are many other cracks in the once solid wall of Darwinian evolution. The idea of "a God of the gaps" is no longer so laughable.

Neither is neo-Darwinism the citadel it once was. "Scientists who reject evolution may be one of the fastest growing minorities ... [who] hold impressive credentials in science" (Larry Hatfield "Educators against Darwin," *Science Digest Special*, Winter 1979, pages 94-96).

> We are sceptical of the claims for the ability of random mutation and natural selection to account for the complexity of life. Careful examination of the evidence for Darwinian theory should be encouraged.
> "A Scientific Dissent from Darwinism," *The Weekly Standard*, October 1, 2001

In 1980 Gould published a paper in a scientific journal predicting the emergence of "a new and general theory of evolution" to replace the neo-Darwinian synthesis. Gould wrote that, though he had been "beguiled" by the unifying power of the Darwinian synthesis when he studied it as a graduate student in the 1960s, the weight of the evidence had driven him to the reluctant conclusion that the synthesis "as a general proposition, is effectively dead, despite its persistence as textbook orthodoxy" (Phillip E. Johnson, *Darwin on Trial*, page 11).

Colin Patterson was senior paleontologist at the British Natural History Museum. He authored the museum's general text on evolution. Here are his words from a recorded lecture:

> Can you tell me anything you know about evolution, any one thing ... that is true? I asked that question of the geology staff at the Field Museum of Natural History, and the only answer I got was silence. I tried it on the members of the Evolutionary Morphology seminar in the University of Chicago, a very prestigious body of evolutionists, and all I got there was silence for a long time.
> "Evolutionism and Creationism," Presentation at the American Museum of Natural History on 5 November 1981

In his classic on evolution Denton wrote: *"Neither of the two fundamental axioms of Darwin's macro-evolutionary theory ... has ... been validated by one single empirical discovery or scientific advance since 1859"* (page 345). Denton has expressed his desire to republish his book, so let no one tell you that he has repudiated his arguments.

Physicist Alan Hayward has devoted many pages in the beginning of his book *Creation and Evolution* to the same situation of growing unbelief in Darwinian evolution. Other books do likewise.

CHAPTER EIGHTEEN SUMMARY:

Ignorant people think all scientists are agreed about evolution. That is not the case. Thousands dispute it, and this chapter has given the evidence.

CHAPTER 19

Creation or Darwinism?

Part three: The evidence from paleontology—1

WOULD IT NOT be helpful if there were one particular branch of knowledge, which falsifies Darwinism so clearly that all who really desire the truth might easily recognize it? There is such—the field of paleontology. Of course we speak of the current situation, not the hopes and despairs of generations of anthropologists. Keep in mind the dictum of Karl Popper that a theory must be falsifiable. If it is not, we should never call it true.

The linchpin of Darwinism is the fossil record of the geologic column. For most secular scientists this is "the life of the party," the final and ultimate court of appeal, for only in the fossil record is there an authentic history of life.

There may be some who are unaware of the fact that evangelical Christians for nearly one and a half centuries have accepted the fact that God "has written the earth's history in indestructible characters on its own rocky bosom; and although the writing had been long unheeded, it has at length attracted the notice of learned and enquiring minds." This comment comes from a learned evangelical source—*The Imperial Bible Dictionary,* article "Creation." The volumes of this set were printed in 1889 and had as their editor the rightly famous Patrick Fairbairn, one of the greatest Bible scholars of the nineteenth century. The geologic column is a reality as sure and true as the rotundity of our earth, and any Christian who denies that fact appropriately invites scornful unbelief.

But the devastating fact that paleontologists have stumbled across is this: *there is no evidence anywhere in the column of a gradual transition from one species to another.* Man, as with all preceding species, turns up as from nowhere. This is the death knell of Darwinism. Darwin's essential thesis was gradualism, and he thought the lack of evidence for that theory was because geology had not yet done a thorough work. He has been proven wrong by 200,000,000 catalogued specimens of about 250,000 fossil species.

Gould comments:

> The absence of fossil evidence for intermediary stages between major transitions in organic design, indeed our inability, even in our imagination, to construct functional intermediates in many cases, has been a persistent and nagging problem for gradualistic accounts of evolution.
> "Is a new and general theory of evolution emerging?" *Paleobiology,* Vol. 6, No. 1, January 1980, page 127

> Gradualists usually extract themselves from the dilemma by invoking the extreme imperfection of the fossil record—if only one step in a thousand survives as a fossil, geology will not record continuous change. ... I reject this argument.
> 'The Return of Hopeful Monsters,' *Natural History,* June-July 1977, pages 22,24

> Darwin's theory of natural selection has always been closely linked to evidence from fossils, and probably most people assume that fossils provide a very important part of the general argument that is made in favour of Darwinian interpretation of the history of life. Unfortunately, this is not strictly true.

> Dr David M. Raup (Curator of Geology, Field Museum of Natural History, Chicago), 'Conflicts between Darwin and paleontology,' *Field Museum of Natural History Bulletin,* Vol. 5, No. 1, January 1979, page 22

Eldredge and Tattersall say the same in *The Myths of Human Evolution,* pages 45-46:

> That individual kinds of fossils remain recognizably the same

throughout the length of their occurrence in the fossil record had been known to paleontologists long before Darwin published his *Origin*. Darwin himself, troubled by the stubbornness of the fossil record in refusing to yield abundant examples of gradual change, devoted two whole chapters to the fossil record. To preserve his argument he was forced to assert that the fossil record was too incomplete, too full of gaps, to produce the expected patterns of change. He prophesied that future generations of paleontologists would fill in these gaps by diligent search and then his major thesis—that evolutionary change is gradual and progressive—would be vindicated. One hundred and fifty years of paleontological research later, it has become abundantly clear that the fossil record will not confirm this part of Darwin's predictions. Nor is the problem a miserably poor record. The fossil record simply shows that this prediction was wrong. ... Only recently has a substantial number of paleontologists blown the whistle.

Now hear from Ager:

> It must be significant that nearly all the evolutionary stories I learned as a student, from Trueman's *Ostrea/Gryphaea* to Carruthers' *Zaphrentis delanouei*, have now been debunked. Similarly, my own experience of more than twenty years looking for evolutionary lineages among the Mesozoic Brachiopoda has proved them equally elusive.
> Dr. Derek V. Ager (Dept. of Geology and Oceanography, University College, Swansea, UK) "The nature of the fossil record," *Proceedings of the Geologists' Association*, Vol. 87, No. 2, 1976, page 132

With the failure of these many efforts science was left in the somewhat embarrassing position of having to postulate theories of living origins, which it could not demonstrate. After having chided the theologian for his reliance on myth and miracle, science found itself in the unenviable position of having to create a mythology of its own: namely, the assumption that what, after long effort, could not be proved to take place today had, in truth, taken place in the primeval past.

Loren Eiseley, Ph.D. (anthropology), "The secret of life," in *The Immense Journey*, page 199

Simpson stated at the 1959 Chicago Centennial celebration for the *Origin of Species* (in *Taxa*, 1960, page 149):

> It is a feature of the known fossil record that most *taxa* appear abruptly. They are not, as a rule, led up to by a sequence of almost imperceptibly changing forerunners such as Darwin believed should be usual in evolution. A great many sequences of two or a few temporally intergrading species are known, but even at this level most species appear without known intermediate ancestors, and really, perfectly complete sequences of numerous species are exceedingly rare. ... These peculiarities of the record pose one of the most important theoretical problems in the whole history of life: is the sudden appearance ... a phenomenon of evolution or of the record only due to sampling bias and other inadequacies?

Paleontologists therefore came to view stasis as just another failure to document evolution. ... Stasis existed in overwhelming abundance, as every paleontologist always knew. But this primary signal of the fourth record, defined as an absence of data from evolution, only highlighted our frustration—and certainly did not represent anything worth publishing. Paleontology therefore fell into a literally absurd vicious circle. No one ventured to document or quantify—indeed, hardly anyone ever bothered to mention or publish it all—the most common pattern in the fossil record: the stasis of most morpho-species throughout their geological duration. All Paleontologists recognise the phenomena, but few scientists write papers about failure to document a desired result.
Stephen Jay Gould, *The Structure of Evolutionary Theory*, pages 745-760 (see also pages 38, 45, 146-155, 990, 1202.)

Chapter Nineteen Summary:

The linchpin of Darwinism is the fossil record. But these days, geologists know that this record does not support Darwinism. The infinite numbers of intermediate species are still "missing links." This evidence is not disputed by anyone reputable.

The pioneers who first published these facts were Steven Jay Gould and Niles Eldredge. They changed the whole scene of science as they broadcast what others knew, but hardly dared voice. Gould in his last days wrote *The Structure of Evolutionary Theory*, in which he frankly tells of the disappointments of paleontologists who looked for evidence in the rocks to support Darwin and found none.

Chapter 20

Creation or Darwinism

Part four: The evidence from Paleontology—2

GOULD'S PROBLEMS WERE not over when he came up with his influential theory. He next proposed along with Eldredge a mechanism called allopatric speciation to explain the rapid generation of new species. Gould was aware that new species would inevitably have to arise in smaller, isolated populations where random processes could have a greater chance of fixing traits. Among those random processes was genetic drift when genetic changes spread or disappear randomly through a population. Thus Gould and Eldredge hoped to explain how evolution could occur in larger, more discrete jumps than Darwinian gradualism predicted. But this too had its problems.

> By relying on the accumulation of new traits within large parent populations, Gould undercut his own rationale for concluding that the fossil record should not preserve many intermediate forms. The reason for this is obvious: if novel genetic traits arise and spread within a large population of organisms, they are more likely to leave behind fossil evidence of their existence. ... Yet the Precambrian fossil record fails to preserve such a wealth of biological experiments during the long periods of relative stability in large populations that Gould's theory envisions. Stephen C. Meyer, *Darwin's Doubt*, page 145

> [The question arises]: If allopatric speciation does not produce fast-acting, trait-generating mechanisms, does species selection? Again the answer is no.
> *Ibid.*, page 147

103

Steven M. Stanley stated that, "despite the detailed study of the Pleistocene mammals of Europe, *not a single valid example is known of phyletic (gradual) transition from one genus to another*" (*Macroevolution: Pattern and Progress*, page 82).

Did you understand that?—not one single valid example of a missing link!

I beg of you not to pass by that last quotation too quickly. Despite the thousands of claims to have found missing links, not one of them has stood the test of time.

> [There is] a great rarity of transitional fossils. This is hardly what one would expect if these transitions were the result of random walks of hundred of undirected mutations in large populations so as to cross the gaps in biological diversity. This should leave the fossil record littered with a multitude of transitional fossils—which we don't find.
> Robert C. Newman, *Three Views on Creation and Evolution*, page 154

Dr. C. Patterson, in a personal letter to Luther D. Sunderland, wrote:

> I fully agree with your comments on the lack of direct illustration of evolutionary transitions in my book. If I knew of any, fossil or living, I would certainly have included them. ... I will lay it on the line—there is not one such fossil for which one could make a watertight argument.
> April 10, 1979

Of course there IS a small handful of alleged intermediates, but these are sharply contested and have no significance when compared with the quarter billion of catalogued fossils. Varieties within species are not new kinds. A hundred different types of dogs still all belong to the canine world. Practising paleontology is far from being a cinch. Consider the following pungent observations:

> The fossil record—in defiance of Darwin's whole idea of gradu-

al change—often makes great leaps from one form to the next. Far from the display of intermediates to be expected from slow advance through natural selection, many species appear without warning. Geology assuredly does not reveal any final graduated organic chain, and this is the most obvious and gravest objection, which can be urged against the theory of evolution.
Steve Jones, *Almost Like a Whale,* page 207

Steve Jones is a devout Darwinist, often quoting the exact words of *The Origin of Species,* and these quotes need to be read in context.

In spite of a century's claims of the discovery of 'missing links,' it is quite possible that *no bone yet found is on the direct genetic line to ourselves.*
page 347

T. H. Huxley, "Darwin's Bulldog," once wrote that if the gaps were a reality through all known time that fact would be fatal to the doctrine of evolution ("Three Lectures on Evolution," September 18, 20, 22, 1876, page 619). Read that again and believe him, as any reasonable person should. Had Huxley known what is well known now he could never have been "Darwin's bulldog."

Well, those gaps ARE a reality, but as Thomas Kuhn has told us, scientific traditions die slowly and only with great reluctance. They are as persistent as erroneous religious traditions.

Why then does the doctrine survive and with dogmatic assertions of certainty? Thomas Kuhn wrote his book, *The Structure of Scientific Revolutions,* to explain this phenomenon. Scientific theories once popular are only slowly released when the evidence against them becomes overwhelming. So it has been, so it is, and so it will be. Remember how long phlogiston, ether, and the steady state of the universe theories lasted. Besides that, for unbelievers in God, there is no other game in town. Huge numbers profess belief in evolution because they cannot entertain the opposite idea—God. Evolution often wins by default.

CHAPTER TWENTY SUMMARY:

Here are more confessions from scientists about the geological evidence against Darwinism. The geologic column reveals that all species arrived abruptly without preceding intermediates, and that they usually remained for millions of years without change. The men quoted are not fundamentalist Christians, but top scientists of great repute.

Chapter 21

Creation or Darwinism

Part five: The Evidence from Paleontology—3

THE LACK OF intermediates has most significance when applied to the appearance of humans. While many fossil hominids have been hailed as our ancestors, none of them has stood the test. Read more on that in a later section.

Mutations make all the difference, or do they?

Neo-Darwinism is a synthesis that accepts the Darwinian doctrine of natural selection. It adds to that its theory regarding mutations, claiming that such can change the DNA and thus ultimately species. Mankind is here, but only supposedly because of a multitude, perhaps an infinite number, of mutations. But while mutations do change genes, the vast proportion of them are deleterious or neutral, and the change is for the worse.

The French science giant, Pierre-Paul Grassé, contended that mutations have no final evolutionary effect because of genetic limitations. He wrote: "No matter how numerous they may be, mutations do not produce any kind of evolution" (see *The Evolution of Living Organisms*, pages 87, 88).

Erwin and Valentine agree:

> Viable mutations with major morphological or physiological effects are exceedingly rare and usually infertile; the chance of two identical rare mutant individuals arising in sufficient propinquity to produce offspring seems too small to consider as a significant evolutionary event.
> "'Hopeful Monsters,' Transposons, and Meazoan Radiation,'

Proceedings of the National Academy of Sciences, Vol. 81, 1984, page 5482

As the mathematicians have insisted, there is just not enough time for chance to evoke all the needed modifications, if single mutations are presumed to be involved and especially when several distinct mutations are needed simultaneously. Even G. G. Simpson, stout Darwinist that he is, agrees that to secure five mutations simultaneously would take forever.
Gordon Rattray Taylor, *The Great Evolution Mystery*, pages 229-230

The word that we find constantly on the lips of Gould and Eldredge is "abrupt." Here is a summary of the way Wm. H. Bird has summarized what most palaeontologists now believe about the abrupt separate arrival of species:

> There is an abrupt appearance for every major stage of Darwinian evolution. That abrupt appearance of complex life characterizes nearly every major category of organisms and every alleged stage in the evolutionary process. Invertebrates (animals without backbones), 'all major invertebrate phyla appear suddenly' and trilobites appear in an 'explosion.' Fish appear abruptly in complex form in the fossil record. ... Reptiles similarly appear abruptly in complex form. ... Birds also appear abruptly in complex form in the fossil record. Mammals appear suddenly in complex form, arising in an 'explosion'. ... Primates appear abruptly in complex form in the fossil record, as acknowledged by Johansen, an evolutionist authority. ... Man, finally, also appears abruptly in complex form. For plants, the same thing is true: 'vascular plants ... arose almost simultaneously.'
> *The Origin of Species Revisited*, Vol. 1, pages 54–56

None of the known fishes is thought to be directly ancestral to the earliest land vertebrates. Most of them lived after the first amphibians appeared, and those that came before show no evidence of developing the stout limbs and ribs that characterize the primitive tetrapods. ... Since the fossil material provides no evidence of other aspects of the transformation from fish to tetrapod, palaeontologists have had to speculate how legs and

aerial breathing evolved.
Barbara J. Stahl (St. Anselm's College, USA) in *Vertebrate History: Problems in Evolution,* pages 148, 195

The [evolutionary] origin of birds is largely a matter of deduction. There is no fossil evidence of the stages through which the remarkable change from reptile to bird was achieved.
W. E. Swinton (British Museum of Natural History, London), *The Origin of Birds,* Chapter 1, in *Biology and Comparative Physiology of Birds,* A. J. Marshall (ed.), Vol. 1, page 1

The explanation of suggested abrupt appearances and systematic gaps ... differs totally between evolutionist and discontinuist scientists. Discontinuist scientists suggest that abrupt appearances and systematic gaps are explained most naturally and logically by discontinuity or unrelatedness of the natural groups of plants and animals.
Ibid., page 50

Despite the bright promise of paleontology providing a means of "seeing" evolution, it has presented some nasty difficulties for evolutionists, the most significant of which is the presence of "gaps" in the fossil record. Evolution requires intermediates between species, and paleontology does not provide them.

Many paleontologists today use the word "mystery" about the coming of mankind, but it is no mystery to those who trust in the opening chapters of Genesis.

CHAPTER TWENTY-ONE SUMMARY:

The chief difference between classic Darwinism and neo-Darwinism is that the latter teaches that DNA changes which we call "mutations" are the main key in evolutionary development. But these days it is widely admitted that most mutations are lethal and that the possibility of getting several "good" mutations in a row is one chance in millions.

CHAPTER 22

Creation or Darwinism?

Part six: Chance, sovereign Lord, or fable?

PATRICK GLYNN, ASSOCIATE director of George Washington University has been well known in Washington DC. Not everybody, however, knows he was once a rabid atheist. He has written a book on his unlearning of the atheism he had gathered at Harvard and Cambridge. It is called *God, the Evidence*. I quote from page 19:

> The past two decades of research have overturned nearly all the important assumptions and predictions of an earlier generation of modern secular and theist thinkers relating to the issue of God. Modern thinkers assumed that science would reveal the universe to be ever more random and mechanical; instead it has discovered unexpected new layers of intricate order that bespeak an almost unimaginably vast master design.

Glynn's first chapter tells of the unveiling of the Anthropic Principle by Brandon Carter, cosmologist of Cambridge University. It was in the year 1973 when many of the world's most eminent astronomers and physicists gathered in Poland to commemorate the 500th birthday of Copernicus. Dozens of lectures were delivered, but only that by Carter has been remembered. The essence of his lecture was that all the myriad laws of the universe had but one objective—to prepare the way for us. This was shocking. No longer could one legitimately believe that man is an unfortunate accident in a backwater of the universe as Bertrand Russell had once claimed. Now it is known that all the fundamental constants such as gravitational force, electro-magnetism, and the strong and the weak nuclear forces have precise values, which if lessened or increased by one in a trillion or more, could return the universe to chaos. Darwin's theory of majestic chance absolutely failed as an explanation of the miracles of existence.

Since then there have been scores of scientific articles and books on the Anthropic Principle. So Dr Antony Flew found his way back to God and with him multitudes of others. Again from Glynn:

> Moderns of the era of Friedrich Nietzsche, and later Bertrand Russell and Sigmund Freud, were convinced that this mechanistic vision of the cosmos was the last word. Neither Russell nor Freud or Marx nor Nietzsche would ever have expected that the mechanistic model itself might be overturned.
> *Ibid.*, page 37

Matthew Fox echoes Glynn:

> When the universe began, about fifteen billion years ago, as a seven-hundred-and-fifty-
> thousand-year fireball that expanded as the universe expanded, there was a decision made in the first second, on our behalf. The decision was that the expansion of the fireball would be at such a rate that, if it were one millionth of a millionth of a millionth of a second slower or faster over seven hundred and fifty thousand years, you and I would not be here today. The earth would not have evolved as the hospitable planet it has.

> It's an awesome story. It makes mystics of everyone. It reminds me of Julian of Norwich's words: 'We have been loved since before the beginning.' This is why physicists are coming out of the closet as mystics. ... Ninety percent of all scientists, I would say, are drawn to science because of the mysticism and the beauty of it.
> "The Mystic in the Machine," *The Future of God,* page 249

Chance (contingency) is clearly not the magic genie, which by waving its wand can bring to pass life, order, animals, man, and mind. The impact of this fact as far as Darwinism is concerned is only beginning to filter down to the multitudes of even educated people. Errors travel around the world while Truth is putting its socks on.

Alan Hayward, in his *Creation and Evolution*, pages 238-239 tells of the recent revolution in science made possible by molecular biology:

> Over the past 25 years, scientists have discovered an exquisite world of nanotechnology within living cells. Inside these tiny labyrinthine enclosures, scientists have found functioning turbines, miniature pumps, sliding clamps, complex circuits, rotary engines, and machines for copying, reading and editing digital information—hardly the simple 'globules of plasma' envisioned by Darwin's contemporaries.

> Moreover, most of these circuits and machines depend on the coordinated function of many separate parts. ... the flagellar motor depends upon the coordinated function of 30 protein parts. Yet the absence of any one of these parts results in the complete loss of motor function. ... The 29- and 28-part versions of this motor do not work. Thus, natural selection can 'select' or preserve the motor once it has arisen as a functioning whole, but it can do nothing to help build the motor in the first place.

Thus Hayward, like Denton and others, rejects the recent attempts to explain away the miracle of the bacterial flagellum. As well try to invent a brain with reasoning and memory. Let the Darwinists start there.

Edmund J. Ambrose, who is a cellular biologist at the University of London warns:

> The difficulties in explaining the origin of increased complexity as a result of bringing a 'cluster' of genes together within the nuclei of a single organism in terms of probabilities, fade into insignificance when we recognize that there must be a close integration of functions between the individual genes of the cluster, which must also be integrated into the development of the entire organism. The improbability increases at an enormous rate as the number of genes increases from one to five. ... The problem of bringing together the five mutated genes we are considering within a single nucleus, and for them to 'fit' immediately into this vast complex of interacting units, is indeed difficult. When it is remembered that they must give some se-

lective advantage, or else become scattered once more within the population at large, due to interbreeding, it seems impossible to explain these events in terms of random mutation alone.
E. A. Ambrose, *The Nature and Origin of the Biological World*, pages 123-4

Denton in his magisterial *Evolution: A Theory in Crisis* has telling words on this matter. We quote him:

> *It is surely a little premature to claim that random processes could have assembled mosquitoes and elephants* when we have to determine the actual probability of the discovery by chance of one single functional protein molecule.
> pages 323–324

In 1979, when *Scientific American* published again the earlier article by George Wald on the certainty that life could arise by chance, it also printed a repudiation. It quoted from Harold Morowitz who had written that "merely to create a bacterium would require more time than the Universe might ever see if chance combinations of its molecules were the only driving force." *Since that time reputable journals have refused to publish articles based on the premise that life arose from chance over billions of years.*

More than a decade earlier there had been an international symposium entitled "Mathematical Challenges to the Neo-Darwinian Interpretation of Evolution," which included not only mathematicians and engineers as participants, but also many leading evolutionary biologists. Again the protest against neo-Darwinism revolved around the issue of randomness. See also what is probably the best book ever written on the early chapters of Genesis, *In the Beginning*, page 226. Henri Blocher rightly points out there that if all came from chance, billions and billions times more time than the billions of earth's history would be required.

All of the preceding helps us to understand the analogy proposed by Hoyle and Wickramasinghe in *Evolution from Space*, page 129:

> The chance that higher life forms might have emerged in this

way is comparable with the chance that 'a tornado sweeping through a junk-yard might assemble a Boeing 747 from the materials therein.'

We have known of the Bronze and Iron Ages. Now we are in what could be called either the Garbage Age or the Information Age. It is full of miracles. A single lily has in its DNA enough storage capacity to store the *Encyclopaedia Britannica* eighty times over. The human brain has the capacity to hold the information equivalent to 20,000,000 books. Again we quote Denton as he comments on the information secreted in minute amounts of DNA:

> The information necessary to specify the design of all the species of organisms which have ever existed on the planet, a number according to G. G. Simpson of approximately one thousand million, could be held in a teaspoon and there would still be room left for all the information in every book ever written. *Ibid.*, page 334

Information is the opposite of chance. It is the product of intelligence and our universe is run by information, i.e., by intelligence. The problems mentioned in the foregoing pages have taxed many scientific brains to breaking point. Goldsmith, a highly esteemed accredited biologist, once listed some of the problems he was contending with and then came up with what has famously become known as the "hopeful monster."

Stephen Jay Gould has recorded how in his graduate days he received and believed the traditional Darwinian doctrine of gradualism. Then came his researches on the fossil column and his discovery that the supposedly infinite number of intermediate forms were just not there. He has also told the story of how discouraging this has proved to many a young paleontologist starting out, even leading to withdrawal and selection of another career. Had the Anthropic Principle appeared earlier, perhaps the whole history of neo-Darwinism might have been different.

Chapter Twenty-two Summary:

A key word used by the world's most well known evolutionist scientist, Stephen Jay Gould, is "contingency" or chance. He says that our arrival is a result of sixty trillion chance events. We have not called on Richard Dawkins as he is widely regarded as a "fundamentalist" in the realm of science. But many other top men in science in view of the Anthropic Principle deny that chance is the key factor in the arrival of the universe, the solar system, and man.

Michael Denton's books—*Evolution: a Theory in Crisis* and *Nature's Destiny: How the laws of biology reveal purpose in the universe*—are very clear in presenting the evidence against the reigning role of chance. See also the many books on the Anthropic Principle. A cell requires the equivalent of 100 million pages of instructions for its formation. Science admits its defeat in providing an explanation for the first life. Only Genesis can solve that problem. If we cannot obtain a single cell by chance, why consider that chance can make both mosquitoes and elephants?

CHAPTER 23

Creation or Darwinism?

Part seven: Hominids and *Homo sapiens*

ALL OF US ARE interested in our supposed animal ancestry, but *after over 150 years of searching there has not been discovered a single fossil that is an undisputed ancestor of man.* Let me expand that claim.

It is now acknowledged that a good deal less is known about Lucy than usually believed. Even its gender is uncertain. Many who read this are familiar with Bill Bryson's *A Short History of Nearly Everything*. His several statements about human origins are impressive. Here are a few:

> Until very recently, it was assumed that we were descended from Lucy and the Laetoli creatures, but now many authorities aren't so sure. ... Not only was Lucy not our ancestor, she wasn't even much of a walker.
> pages 393-394

> The first modern humans are surprisingly shadowy. We know less about ourselves, curiously enough, than about almost any other line of hominids. It is odd indeed, as Tattersall notes, that 'the most recent major events in human evolution—the emergence of our own species—is perhaps the most obscure of all. Nobody can ever quite agree where truly modern humans first appear in the fossil record.'
> page 404

> Modern human beings show remarkably little genetic variability—'there's more diversity in one social group of fifty-five chimps than in the whole human population. ... We are recently

descended from a small founding population.'
page 410

Distinguished physicist, Gerald L. Schroeder, in his *The Science of God* says:

> We may never know the full truth of our origins. No less an authority than Ernst Mayr, professor emeritus of zoology at Harvard University, former curator of the American Museum of Natural History, an avowed lifelong advocate of Darwinian evolution, has finally come to admit that the origin of our species is a 'puzzle' (to use his word) that may never be solved.
> page 127

Mayr has a lot of scientific company. Many have used terms similar to "puzzle" when discussing the origin of mankind. "Mystery" is a much-used word. Consider these lines from Michael Denton, a man I greatly respect, having shared a lecture platform with him some years ago:

> The 'mystery of mysteries'—the origin of new beings on earth—is still largely as enigmatic, as when Darwin set sail on the Beagle. *Evolution: a Theory in Crisis*, page 359

The most famous "human" fossil is, of course, the Piltdown man presented by the experts to generations of scientists as the genuine article, and then in the 1950s it was discovered to be a hoax. Himmelfarb comments:

> The zeal with which eminent scientists defended it, the facility with which even those who did not welcome it managed to accommodate to it, and the way in which the most respected scientific techniques were soberly and painstakingly applied to it, with the apparent result of confirming both the genuineness of the fossils and the truth of evolution, are at the very least suspicious. *Darwin and the Darwinian Revolution*, pages 310-11

The Nebraska man was a gross misinterpretation built on the slender evidence of a tooth, which turned out to be merely a pig's tooth. As can readily be conjectured the problem with many paleontologists is that they are so determined to find a human ancestor that any scrap of bone can easily be labelled as a great hominid discovery.

Solly Zuckerman, long-time departmental chairman of the British Advisory Council on Science Policy, has this to say:

> The (fossil) record is so astonishing that it is legitimate to ask whether much science is yet to be found in this field at all. The study of the Piltdown man provides a pretty good answer.
> *Beyond the Ivory Tower*, 1970, page 64

> So much glamour still attaches to the theme of the missing link, and to man's relationships with the animal world, that it may always be difficult to exorcize from the comparative study of primates, living and fossil, the kind of myths, which the unaided eye is able to conjure out of a well of wishful thinking.
> *Ibid.*, pages 93-94

Richard Leakey discovered a skull (1970) older than Australopithecines, Java man (Peking man) and concluded, "Either we toss out this skull or we toss out our theories of early man" ("Skull 1470—New Clue to Earliest Man?", *National Geographic*, Vol. 143, page 819).

The Java man fragments discovered by Eugene Dubois have now been renamed as *Homo erectus*, but that classification is now considered as but a class of *Homo sapiens*.

Another skull discovered by Shipman "reduced all our nicely organized constructs to a rubble" ("Baffling Limb on the Family Tree," *Discover*, Sep. 1986, page 87f.).

Pithecanthropus we now know was never a man, only a gibbon. William Fix has before his first chapter a list of the once hailed ancestors of man that have one by one been repudiated. The Neanderthals are now accepted as truly human and so have the Cro-Magnons. And this despite the bad press the former received for decades.

> Hill, anthropologist of Harvard, scathingly asserted: 'Compared to other sciences, the mythic element is greatest in paleoanthropology.'

Richard Dawkins has recently written *The Greatest Show on Earth* and he has a chapter entitled "Missing Persons? Missing no Longer," pages 183-207. This is a really amazing chapter. He makes claim after claim that leading paleoanthropologists would reject. It is as though he has given up reading the literature.

Dawkins on pages 188-189 waxes enthusiastic over Lucy (*Australopithecus afarensis*) and claims she walked upright on the ground. This is just not true.

Ian Tattersall, probably the most well known man in his field, in his *The Monkey in the Mirror* has this to say:

> It wasn't long before various scientists began to point out anatomical characteristics in *A. afarensis* that were not concordant with a fully human-like pattern of locomotion. … Soon there was a small industry devoted to showing that for example, the long curved hand and feet bones, the conical trunk, and the short hind limbs of *afarensis* would not only have been a handicap when moving on the ground, but would have been an asset when feeding and moving in the trees.
> *The Monkey in the Mirror*, pages 87-88

Does this mean that *afarensis* walked upright in the way that we do? Here the answer is certainly negative. … among all the noisy competing claims, one thing is pretty sure: Lucy and her kind did not locomote in anything like the modern human fashion.

"Lucy does not represent an ephemeral waypoint along the journey from ape to human" (*Ibid*, pages 88-89).

How is it that Dawkins, who must have read this book (so pertinent to his claims), denies what the experts say? Pages could here be devoted to showing that what is true of Dawkins' use of Lucy is also true of his other "evidences" of the supposed forerunners of *Homo sapiens*.

It must be admitted that our knowledge of the first humans is far from complete. Many things have been said and continue to be said on both sides that are false. For example, for a long time it was taken for granted that *Homo erectus* was distinct from modern man and his predecessor. Now it is acknowledged that the differences are no more pronounced than seen between different modern races such Eskimos and Bushmen. Professor William Laughlin from the University of Connecticut made extensive anatomical examinations of the natives of the Aleutian islands and became aware that the people he examined were very similar to what was known of *Homo erectus.*

May I now underline that man's abrupt appearance is characteristic of the coming of each new kind? There is not just one missing link—they are innumerable. In this man is not a *sui generis.* Because all other species have suddenly been manifested it is to be expected that it would be the same way with man. He, like them, comes as out from nowhere and comes to stay. The neo-Darwinian offer of mutations as the source of new information for new species does not hold water.

An agnostic physicist and Fellow of the Royal Society, to whom the theory of creation is "anathema," recently concluded that the scientific evidence better supports that theory than evolution:

> I think, however, that we must go further than this and admit that the only acceptable explanation is creation. I know that this is anathema to physicists, as indeed it is to me, but we must not reject a theory that we do not like if the experimental evidence supports it.
> Wm. R. Bird, *Origin of Species Revisited,* page 45

> The frequency with which a *single non-harmful mutation* is known to occur is about 1 in 1000. The *probability that two* favourable mutations would occur is one in 10 to the third, *1 in a million. ...* It is most *unlikely that* fewer than five genes *could ever be involved* in the formation of even the simplest new structure, previously unknown to the organism. The probability now becomes *one in one thousand million million.* We already know that *mutations in living cells appear once in ten million to once in one hundred thousand million.* It is evident that the probability of five favourable mutations occurring within a single life

cycle of an organism is *effectually zero.*
E. J. Ambrose, *The Nature and Origin of the Biological World,*
page 120

According to George Wald:

> If you make a rough estimate. ... it looks as if something of the
> order of ten million years is needed to establish a mutation. ...
> That is, each of these single amino acid changes appears rel-
> atively frequently in individuals as pathology, but to establish
> one such characteristic in a species seems to take something of
> the order of 10 million years. To establish one such change as a
> regular characteristic in a species seems to take something of the
> order of 10 million years.
> "Discussion," in Paul S. Moorhead and Martin M. Kaplan (eds),
> *Mathematical Challenges to the Neo-Darwinian Interpretation of*
> *Evolution,* page 19

> Paleontology is now looking at what it actually finds, not what
> it is told it is supposed to find. As is now well known, *most fossil*
> *species appear instantaneously* in the record, persist for some mil-
> lions of years *virtually unchanged, only to disappear abruptly—the*
> *'punctuated equilibrium* pattern of Eldredge and Gould.'
> Tom Kemp, "A fresh look at the fossil record," *New Scientist,* 5
> Dec. 1985, pages 65-66

Human Origins is a very recent book by well-known paleoanthropologists setting forth the orthodox neo-Darwinian viewpoint. Here
are some quotations that should be of interest to readers on both
sides, but note that the usual claim is that advanced late hominids
have existed for about five million years. However, hominids are
not necessarily humans. Even monkeys and apes can perform some
primitive activities similar to human procedures. The human brain
distinguishes *Homo sapiens* from all supposed predecessors. And
unlike animal forms fossil evidence for the evolution of a brain with
our human qualities cannot and does not exist.

We must ever keep in mind that the struggle between the original
apostate, Satan, and God, was just as real before the Fall as after. The

whole paleontological record testifies to that. There can be no doubt that Satan did his best to counterfeit the humans he knew God would make.

As to when 'hominids' become 'people,' well you just pays your money and takes your choice.
Rob DeSalle and Ian Tattersall, *Human Origins, What Bones and Genomes Tell Us About Ourselves,* page 47

When we began our careers as scientists we never realized that philosophy would be such a huge part of our everyday work.
Ibid., page 11

What is it about our human nature that makes us wonder about where we came from? We need only to look upward at the sky or downward to the ground to be puzzled, amazed, and inquisitive about our and their existence. But how did we achieve the ability to wonder about our place in nature and in the universe?
Ibid., page 12

The recently discovered cave paintings at Chauvet, France, and the more famous but younger ones of Lascaux in France and Altamira and El Castillo in Spain, are but a few examples of amazing and extremely beautiful depictions of animals from the period between about 34,000 and 10,000 years ago. ...

There can be little question that the people who quested in this way 30,000 years ago were able to think not only about a plethora of practical subjects, but about abstract concepts, such as their existence on this planet and their place in nature. In this fundamental sense, these people were modern people.
Ibid.

It is amazing that, of the many civilizations that have left or are continuing to leave records of their thought processes, almost all have bequeathed us evidence of their interest in their own origins.
Ibid.

Darwin personally found the results of his novel thought pro-

cesses excruciating. ... It felt like 'confessing a murder.'
Ibid., page 18

Paleontology, as we know it today, is only as old as our father's toolboxes—less than half a century.
Ibid., page 22

Exactly what goes on inside the brain to produce what we experience as consciousness remains mysterious after well over a century of research.
Ibid., page 169

But to us, the difference that really matters is that we are capable of thinking abstract thoughts, and of talking about them. ...

As far as we can tell, the kind of intelligence we have is different from that of any other living animal species, including some of our extinct relatives. None of them made paintings or sculptures. And most likely, smart as they were, they didn't tell each other stories, either.
Ibid.

We human beings are most profoundly set off from the rest of Nature in being symbolic creatures.
Ibid., page 191

Natural selection is not a creative force; it cannot call the new into existence in a relentless drive toward optimization. ... It can only work with what is there already.
Ibid., page 192

Still, even with the new knowledge it is not particularly easy to interpret. ... Problems in interpreting the fossil record are legion.
Ibid., page 192

We are, then, separated from the rest of Nature by a profound cognitive chasm.
Ibid., page 191

So while ... the archaeological record gives us only the most incomplete perspective of the evolution of technologies, the situation is very much worse when we approach the area of cognition. ... Thoughts and perceptions aren't [preserved], or at least they weren't until the invention of writing, a mere 5,000 years ago. We thus have to read mental processes from the most indirect evidence, and even then we can be sure of nothing. *Ibid.*, page 194

It is arguable whether we can read symbolic thought (as distinguished from advanced intuitive processes) from any aspect of the stone tool record, and the few cases of claimed early symbolism in Africa are all debated.
page 198

What we can predict, however, is that 40 years from now, the human fossil record will look very different from what we think we know today. When we became involved in evolutionary biology 30 or 40 years ago, ... the picture that most scholars derived from it was very different from the signal we are getting today. Science, as we have said, is a system of provisional knowledge, and it is inconceivable that several decades hence our understanding of the human past will not make our present viewpoints look quaint and naive.
page 204

Why so much confusion and disagreement and debate? Because the problems are many and because of the nature of the human animal or species. Cognitive dissonance and deliberate choice play their part. These factors affect both Creationists (those who believe in an earth up to 10,000 years old, and a universal flood as the cause of the geologic column) and Darwinists. The former ignore the visible evidence of thousands of oil wells in USA. And the fruitage of millions of dollars spent in geological research. Thousands of geologists tell the same story. As for the second group the "impossibility" of God, and professional coercion have inevitable influence. *Theophobia is a very dangerous disease.*

Chapter Twenty-three Summary:

After the finding of Skull 1470, Richard Leakey made one of the most revealing statements concerning the supposed evolution of man from apes. In an interview he said:

> Either we toss out this skull or we toss out our theories of early man. It simply fits no previous models of human beginnings. ... [it] leaves in ruins the notion that all early fossils can be arranged in an orderly sequence of evolutionary chance.
> *National Geographic,* Vol. 143, No. 6, June 1973, page 819

In 1978 Dr. Richard Leakey and Roger Lewin wrote *People of the Lake.* Observe the confession on page 19:

> What the fossils tell us directly, of course, is what our ancestors and their close relatives looked like. Or rather, to be more accurate, they give us some clues about the appearance of early hominids, because until someone is lucky enough to come across a complete skeleton of one of our ancestors, much of what we say about them is pure inference, guesswork.
>
> The main problem in reconstructing the origins of man is lack of fossil evidence: all there is could be displayed on a dinner table.
> "Was Darwin Right: Chance or Design?" *New Scientist,* 20 May 1982, page 491

CHAPTER 24

Creation or Darwinism?

Part eight: The conclusions of paleontologists

Perhaps the most up to date reliable presentation of the fossil hominid record is the recent four-volume set *The Human Fossil Record*, printed by Wiley-Liss over several years at the beginning of this century and written by Ian Tattersall and Jeffrey Schwartz. It is described by Amazon as "the most authoritative and comprehensive documentation of the fossil evidence relevant to the study of our evolutionary past." In the Overview at the close of the fourth volume, Tattersall sums up:

> The search for a direct personal ancestor of *Homo sapiens* is in many ways so frustrating. ... *Homo sapiens* appears to be an outlier among all the hominid forms we have examined. ...

> Our science still labours beneath the heavy hand of the received wisdom that is becoming threadbare as an organizing paradigm. There is no doubt in our minds that if the hominid fossil record that has been laboriously unearthed over the last 150 years were to be discovered all at once tomorrow, the resulting picture of hominid phylogeny would look completely different to any that students are taught today ... we thus do not claim any definiteness for the rudimentary awareness that we have developed of the morphological complexities that characterize the history of the hominid family. ... we do believe that many familiar paleoanthropic systematic constructs have outlived their usefulness. It is becoming clearer that any substantial progress in paleoanthropology will involve abandoning traditional scenarios of human evolution, and require rethinking the structure of the human fossil record from the ground up. Tinkering in our view will not do the

trick. *It is at the very least clear that the systematic framework that currently underpins our notion of human evolution is inadequate ... some at least of what we believe today is wrong ...* despite rumours to the contrary none of us is writing for the ages.
[Jeffrey H. Schwartz and] Ian Tattersall, *The Human Fossil Record, Craniodental morphology of early hominids (genera Australopthicus, Paranthropus, Orrorin) and overview,* Vol. 4, pages 510-511

Put with that honest confession Ian Tattersall's comments in *The Monkey in the Mirror* and *The Fossil Trail.* On the paper cover of the former is found these words: "Evolutionary theory isn't a finite set of conclusions based on overwhelming evidence. It is our evolving effort to make sense out of a handful of incomplete fossil remains." Please note that the fossil evidence is described this century as a "handful." Some have denied the earlier statements by scientists that all the fossil evidence for human ancestors could be put on a billiard table, in a pick-up truck, or in a coffin. But the last word is a " handful." It is true that there are museums with whole rooms of fossils, but they are not filled by hominids. On pages 37-38 of this book we read:

> If the transformational notion were accurate, histories of continuity should clearly show up in the structure of the paleontological record. Yet, if the truth be told, the fossils themselves had never really borne out this expectation. ... What we don't often see, however, is compelling evidence of the gradual transition of one species into another.

On page 146 are these words, "Fossils of hominids ... are fairly thin on the ground, and their analysis has been handicapped by an excessively simplistic view of morphology."

And on page 141:

> With the arrival on Earth of symbol-centered, behaviourally modern *Homo sapiens,* an entirely new order of being had materialized on the scene. And explaining just how this extraordinary new phenomenon came about is at the same time both the most

intriguing question, and the most baffling one, in all of biology.

In 2009 *The Fossil Trail* appeared by the same author. It is similarly straightforward. On page 275, the following appears:

> I don't pretend that what you have read in this book is objective history in the strictest sense; it is simply the perception of one active practitioner of the science of paleoanthropology ... what we think today depends very largely on what we thought yesterday. If the entire human fossil record were to be discovered tomorrow and to be studied by experienced paleontologists who had developed their skills in the absence of any preconceptions about human origins, I am pretty sure that (after the inevitable bout of intellectual indigestion) a range of interpretations would emerge that is very different from what is on offer now.

On page 177, Tattersall tells us that the much-touted Turkana boy was "very much like the people who live around Lake Turkana today." In other words, he was truly human, with "an essentially modern human anatomy." He was clearly "an upright strider." But in *Human Origins* DeSalle and Tattersall give a different view with the Turkana boy less than human.

An earlier volume co-authored with Niles Eldredge is similarly informative. Here are a few snippets:

> Find enough fossils, it is believed, and the course of evolution will somehow be revealed. But if this were really so, one could confidently expect that as more hominid fossils were found the story of human evolution would become clearer. Whereas, if anything, the opposite has occurred. ... The fossil history of life is something that cannot be directly discovered. ... Our lives would be greatly simplified if we could just draw lines on a time chart to join up earlier fossils with later ones in a progressive sequence. Unfortunately, we can't. ...

> With the spotty evidence at our disposal we can construct an almost unlimited number of scenarios to account for the final arrival on earth of modern man, and at this point we are unable

to make clear choices between any of them. The general pattern, if you wish *is* chaos.
The Myths of Human Evolution, pages 127, 155

We can take our pick—the inspired Word of God, or the fallible changeable word of brilliant men.

Another recent work, this one by Robert Wenke, entitled *Patterns in Prehistory*, tells us that all modern discussions on human origins "reveal profoundly different conclusions ... the scholars disputing everything" (page 205).

Chapter Twenty-four Summary:

Pronouncements by world-respected, twenty-first century paleontologists boldly declare that our present views will change drastically in coming years, and that all we have at present regarding human origins is a "handful" of fossils differently interpreted.

Charles Darwin stated:

> The number of intermediate varieties, which have formerly existed on the earth [must] be truly enormous ["innumerable", pages 154, 231]. Why then is not every geological formation and every stratum full of such intermediate links? Geology assuredly does not reveal any such finely graduated organic chain; and this, perhaps, is the most obvious and gravest objection which can be waged against my theory.
> *On the Origin of Species,* page 251

Michael Denton comments:

> What they [the rocks] have never yielded is any of Darwin's myriads of transitional forms. Despite the tremendous increase in geological activity in every corner of the globe and despite the discovery of many strange and hitherto unknown forms, the infinitude of connecting links has still not been discovered and the fossil record is about as discontinuous as it was when Darwin was writing the *Origin*. The intermediates have remained as elusive as ever.
> Michael Denton, *Evolution: A Theory in Crisis,* page 162

I defy anyone to read Denton's chapter "The Fossil Record," free from bias, without coming to his conclusions which completely nullify Darwin's theories about the origin of man.

CHAPTER 25

The Historicity of Adam—the First Man

SO WHERE DOES all this leave Adam?—*exactly where Scripture places him.* He is presented as the climax of God's work of Creation. He is a key theological element in the Genesis story, because the Fall underlies all else in Scripture. See Luke 3:37-38; Romans 5:14-19; 1 Corinthians 15:22, 1 Timothy 2:13-14 and Jude 14 for the historicity of Adam.

Consider this frank but significant boast of a well-known American atheist:

> It becomes clear then that the whole justification of Jesus' life and death is predicated on the existence of Adam and the forbidden fruit he and Eve ate. Without the original sin who needs to be redeemed? Without Adam's fall into a life of constant sin terminated by death, what purpose is there to Christianity? None!
> G. Richard Bozarth, "The Meaning of Evolution," *American Atheist,* September 20, 1979

The Hebrew word for Adam is used both for mankind and for the individual of the early Genesis account. See Genesis 1:26–27; 5:1-3. But, after Genesis 11, that word is never used in the next 39 chapters—except in one verse (Genesis 16:12), where it is part of a descriptive metaphor. In the first eleven chapters the Hebrew word for "man" (Adam) appears about 45 times. Those first chapters revolve around all of history prior to Abraham and encompass the whole world. But after the Tower of Babel the scene shrinks. It is no longer global but restricted to the Promised Land of the patriarchs and nearby geographical areas.

After Genesis 3:24 we have a huge swathe of human history omitted by the Genesis writer because God knew it was not pertinent for his initial readership. In that missing period one could posit that our earliest ancestors appear, Adam's descendants, the Neanderthals and the Cro-Magnons (and possibly some before the Neanderthals), truly human, and truly part of our lineage. (Earth's population at that time was probably very tiny.) Genesis 4 begins again with a later man who is also called Adam because that word means "man." And his wife has the same name as the earlier Eve long before. Thus the continuity of chapters three and four is preserved.

It may help to remember statements from Kidner and Foster:

> If Genesis is abbreviating a long history, the sheer vastness of the ages it spans ... is not so sharp a problem as the fact that *almost the whole of this immensity lies, for the palaeontologist, between the first man and the first farmer—that is ... between Adam and Cain, or even between Adam inside and outside Eden.*
> Derek Kidner, *Genesis*, page 27

> The formulation used to denote Adam throughout the first three chapters of Genesis is *Ha Adam. But that, in Hebrew, is not a personal name at all. It simply means 'the human.'* 'Adam' is not used as a given name, to denote a particular individual, until chapter 4. Throughout the stories of the creation and the 'Fall,' Adam is expressly and deliberately a generic human.
> Charles Foster, *The Selfless Gene*, page 129

Without pressing Foster's comments too closely his main idea is invaluable. In Genesis chapters 1-3 Adam *is* a particular person, but also generic man in the sense of the Head of the race whose Fall would affect all later generations. Between that Adam and the Adam of Genesis 4 is a vast period of time, which God deliberately leaves undiscussed because it is of no value to his people until modern times.

It is worthwhile comparing the King James version of Genesis 2:19 and 3:8 with those verses in most modern versions such as the Revised Standard version or the Jerusalem Bible. The latter in Genesis 1-3 do not use the proper name but rather "the man." This is of great significance. We do not read in the first three chapters that God called the first man by a name. That is delayed until chapter 4. The man of chapters 1-3 preceded the Adam of chapter four by a long period. The eleven uses of Adam in the KJV are all mistranslations.

It is not without significance that the geography of Eden is beyond precise location. Wenham suggests: "Maybe the insoluble geography is a way of saying that it is now inaccessible to, even unlocatable by, later man" (pages 66-67). The Eden the first Adam knew is unbelievably distant in time and location from the place where Cain and Abel fought. Everything told about it removes it from the experiences of people recorded in the fourth chapter and beyond. Sensing this fact Richardson writes:

> Attempts to locate a geographical site of Eden are as foolish as trying to identify the spot on the road from Jerusalem to Jericho where the traveller was attacked by robbers in the parable of the Good Samaritan.
> *Genesis I-XI,* page 62

Similar folly has often been manifested by devout seekers after the ark on the mountains of Ararat.

It is not unknown for Bible writers to leave out significant passages of time if time is not pertinent to their objectives. Between Ezra 6 and 7 lie scores of years unmentioned and ignored. In the Gospels apart from the incident of the Christ child at the Temple about thirty years are passed by. Genesis 4 speaks of Adam becoming the father of Cain and Abel as key figures in the downward march to the universal flood. But we are to remember that the name Adam just means "man" and need not be identified with the man of the preceding three chapters.

Genesis chapters 1-3 have no chronological points after Creation and, after the pictorial paradise, geography lapses to be taken up again in chapter four. Now we find hints of a world much more populated than in chapter 3. Cain is afraid of being killed by some stranger and he marries and builds a city. The only way we can preserve the theological teaching of Genesis is to recognize that the inspired writer has not said anything about the long period when humans existed after the original Adam (man) of Genesis 1-3. Moses knew nothing about these and God did not tell him. Between Genesis 3 and 4 lie many thousands of years of human existence, and include people such as Neanderthals and Cro-Magnons who sprang from Adam the first. It is not surprising that the first references to industry and the arts are found only in chapter 4 and beyond. The Adam of chapters 1-3 knew nothing about these.

We are compelled by paleontology and geology to acknowledge the great age of our globe (about 4.5 billion years) and the considerable age of mankind—most estimates range from about 30,000 to 150,000 years—years occupied chiefly perhaps by the Neanderthals and the Cro-Magnons. And the best way to explain the evidence of humans being last in the geologic column is probably Progressive Creationism, which seems more than hinted at by the abrupt appearance of each species, sometimes after huge eras of time. Man's appearance also was abrupt, and not preceded by fossil men (each of which has known notoriety and then bit the dust). But Genesis 4 with its beginning of cities dates about 10,000 B.C.

God by creative fiat brought life into existence, and then at appropriate times his touch or mere will brought the required changes for the abrupt appearances of new species. Finally, Genesis 1:26-28 was fulfilled in God's creation of Adam and Eve. Many have seen this and names known to us today include Bernard Ramm, Alan Hayward, Richard Newman, Hugh Ross, and so on.

It must be plainly stated that our knowledge of the first humans is very slight. We cannot be dogmatic about the predecessors of the Neanderthals. But, however far back humans go, Adam was their source. Keep in mind that the creation of all things took place over thirteen billion years ago if we include the universe, and about four and half billion years for this planet. But Genesis 1 says nothing about the primeval ages. While most readers of the Bible's first chapter have jumped to the conclusion that it had reference to about 10,000 years or less, the facts are otherwise. Genesis 1 points back billions of years. But Genesis 4 belongs to about 10,000 years ago. So it is not to be wondered at if God's climactic creative act, man, also belongs to a time buried in obscurity. Through all of Scripture it is clear that God's chief intent was not to educate us in secular matters. His aim has always been our spiritual maturity. All the teachings of Christ confirm this fact. As regards hominids keep in mind the verdict of Harvard zoologist Richard Lewontin: "No fossil hominid species can be established as our direct ancestor" (*Human Diversity*, page 163). Henry Gee, editor of *Nature* would agree. Thus he says: "Fossil evidence of human evolutionary history is fragmentary, and open to various interpretations" ("Return to the Planet of the Apes," *Nature*, Vol. 412, 12 July 2001, pages 131–132). Looking at the "evidence" from the standpoint of the twenty-first century, Gee declares it would all fit in a small box.

May I repeat in a nutshell what the preceding paragraphs endeavour to say? The idea of an Adam who lived ages ago is very hard for us to comprehend, but the fact that Genesis 1 is telling of a creation that took place over thirteen billion years ago should help us. The Adam figure follows after the ancient creation with its progressive creation of ascending life forms and thus his great antiquity is not to be wondered at. When one reads very thoughtfully the first three chapters of the Bible, they convey a consciousness that what we have here is suprahistorical. These chapters are elevated far above anything we know in human history. They belong to a pristine era with which we are uninformed. Consider the tremendous difference between these chapters and the civilization presented in the chapter that follows (chapter 4). In chapter four we have a city, technology, culture, music, and so on—see the last verses of the chapter. What a tremendous gap this creates between itself and the preceding chapters! It was God's intention that the meaning of this gap should become apparent only when it was needed—in the era dominated by modern science.

We must be very clear about our options. If we eviscerate Adam and the Fall, everything else is flux. Darwin's *Origin of Species* accomplished this for the modern world, turning it into a mainly pagan civilization with few reserves against despair, licentiousness, and violence. Consider the frank avowal of Dr. Will Provine, Professor of Biological Sciences, at Cornell University:

There are no gods, no purposes, no goal-directed forces of any kind. There is no life after death. When I die, I am absolutely certain that I am going to be dead. That's the end for me. There is no ultimate foundation for ethics, no ultimate meaning to life, and no free will for humans, either.

"Darwinism: Science or Naturalistic Philosophy?" A debate between William B. Provine and Phillip E. Johnson at Stanford University, 30 April 1994

He did not realize that he was using his free will to choose a series of errors. Now contrast the sanity of C. S. Lewis:

> There are all sorts of reason for believing in God, and here I will mention only one. Supposing there was no intelligence behind the universe, no creative mind. In that case nobody designed my brain for the purpose of thinking. It is merely that when the atoms inside my skull happen for physical or chemical reasons to arrange themselves in a certain way, this gives me as a by-product, the sensation I call thought. But if so, how can I trust my own thinking to be true? It is like upsetting a milk-jug and hoping that the way the splash arranges itself will give you a map of London. But if I cannot trust my own thinking, of course I cannot trust the arguments leading to atheism, and therefore the reason to be an atheist, or anything else. Unless I believe in God, I cannot believe in thought or anything else: so I can never use thought to disbelieve in God.
>
> *The Case for Christianity*, page 32

The alternative to Adam is Darwin's evolution, which teaches that everything, our religion, our ethics, our loves and hates, all that we consider to be true, is the product of chance. *But there is absolutely no good reason to accept Darwinism.*

Chapter Twenty-five Summary:

The Bible is both clear and definite about the facticity of Adam and Eve, our first parents. Paul's whole argument in Romans 5 is based on this reality. See also the genealogy of Luke 3 and 1 Corinthians 15:22 as well as the early chapters of Genesis. However, it is important that we understand what Derek Kidner and others are trying to tell us about Adam. Here is one significant quotation from a very respected Christian scholar:

> If Genesis is abbreviating a long history, the sheer vastness of the ages it spans ... is not so sharp a problem as the fact that almost the whole of this immensity lies, for the paleontologist, between the first man and the first farmer—that is, between Adam and Cain, or even between Adam inside and outside Eden. Derek Kidner, *Genesis*, page 27

There is a tremendous difference between the milieu of Genesis chapters 2 and 3 and that of chapter 4. The latter has a city and technology, and multitudes of people of whom Cain is afraid. But the preceding chapters are pristine, altogether different, and the Adam of Genesis 1-3 is different from the Adam of chapter 4. The Hebrew word for Adam just means "man." In Genesis 1-3 the Hebrew word is usually prefaced by the article, which is not chiefly the case in the following chapters of Genesis. The only way to solve the problems created by the vast age of the world and Bible history is to recognize the gap between the end of chapter 3 and the beginning of chapter 4. The Adam of chapters 1-3 is prehistory whereas the Adam of chapter 4 onwards lives in a world of about ten thousand years ago. The Adam of chapter 4 is a different man.

CHAPTER 26

Progressive Creationism

WHEN WE SPEAK of primeval time and the creative work of God, metaphors must be invoked. As the last book of the Bible peeps into the very distant future it employs symbols throughout, and similarly when the Bible's first book looks at the distant past it too invokes a measure of picture language. Remember, God's works are just as mysterious as God himself. If we knew all the answers we would be God. Many scientists believe that the progressive development of living creatures has been due to a built-in directive such as is found in every seed. From the time of Augustine some Christians have so believed. The Christian must go further. He believes the whole Trinity had a share in Creation, and that the work of the Holy Spirit is ever as the Creator and giver of life. "Thou sendest forth thy spirit and they are created" (Psalm 104:30).

Christians who hold to the doctrine of the Trinity believe both in the transcendence and the immanence of God. Consider the words of Jürgen Moltmann:

> The Trinitarian concept of creation binds together God's transcendence and his immanence. The one-sided stress on God's transcendence in relation to the world led to Deism, as with Newton. The one-sided stress on God's immanence in the world led to pantheism, as with Spinoza. The Trinitarian concept of creation integrates the elements of truth in monotheism and pantheism. ... God, having created the world, also dwells in it, and conversely the world, which he has created exists in him. This is a concept which can really only be thought and described in Trinitarian terms.
> *God in Creation,* page 98

The *New Dictionary of Theology* (IVP) states, "Moltmann combines a creative faithfulness to the central themes of biblical and historical Christianity," but we need not accept Moltmann's particular view on the Trinity to acknowledge the biblical sense of immanence.

Langdon Gilkey in *Maker of Heaven and Earth* speaks similarly:

> In describing the character of 'creatures,' we have said that although their existence is real enough, nevertheless it is a completely dependent existence. Their being has come to them, not from their own nature, but from beyond themselves in God, whose creative act brought them into being. They *are*, then, only so long as God's creative act continues to give them being, for they do not generate their own power to be from themselves, but as the moments of their existence pass, they receive it continually from beyond themselves. The renewal of each creature in each succeeding moment of its existence is a victory of being over the non-being of temporal passage. In the onrush of temporal passage, this victorious recreation in the next moment is accomplished by a power beyond ourselves, since each creature is caught within the present and cannot establish itself beyond the present.

> Thus, without the continuing power of God each creature would lapse back into the non-being from whence it came. Were God to cease to be in things, they would simply cease to be. In speaking, therefore, of creatures as continually dependent upon their Creator for their existence, the doctrine of creation implies the continual immanence of God in all His creatures as firmly as it asserts His transcendence over them. For this reason the concept of God's continuing creation of the world in each succeeding moment of its passage is the ground for the further doctrine of God's providential rule over each aspect of creation and each moment of its duration. God is immanent in all things as the creative and preserving power in which all exists. ... No one has phrased this paradox of immanence and transcendence better than Athanasius: 'Within all according to His goodness and power, yet without all in His proper nature.' ...

The Christian doctrine of God as Creator and Redeemer invariably connects both transcendence and immanence, and can safely lose neither one.
pages 106–109

We moderns distinguish between the natural and the supernatural. Such is not the view of either the Old or New Testament. God is in all things, either creatively to sustain, or permissively to allow decay and death. Every breath is his gift, as is every moment of existence. Remember Daniel 5:23: "the God in whose hand your breath is."

We who do not know one millionth of the mysteries hidden in a blade of grass or in a human seed of life are very presumptuous if we claim to fully understand the mighty acts of God.

"The secret things belong to the Lord our God, but the things revealed belong to us and our children forever, that we may follow the words of this law" (Deut. 29:29).

"For now we see through a glass darkly." "Now I know in part" (1 Cor. 13:12).

"As you do not know the path of the wind, or how the body is formed in a mother's womb, so you cannot understand the work of God, the Maker of all things" (Eccl. 11:5).

Genesis uses anthropomorphic terms when speaking of divine actions, and this was fully appropriate in speaking to finite man. But the Bible's revelation of God as omnipresent, omniscient, and omnipotent teaches us that God needs only to will a thing and it is. He does not need to speak or to fashion. The Genesis picture of the Almighty taking six days to create the universe is similar to the picture of a very tall man bending down to lisp to a tiny child. It showed infinite condescension by a loving heavenly Father who wished to offer an example to creatures who needed both work and rest in regular rhythm. Psalm 139 has insights that we must take very seriously as we consider God's miraculous work in creation.

O Lord, you have searched me and you know me. You know

when I sit and when I rise; you perceive my thoughts from afar. You discern my going out and my lying down; you are familiar with all my ways. Before a word is on my tongue, you know it completely, O Lord.

You hem me in—behind and before; you have laid your hand upon me. Such knowledge is too wonderful for me, too lofty for me to attain.

Where can I go from your Spirit? Where can I flee from your presence: If I go up to the heavens, you are there; if I make my bed in the depths, you are there. If I rise on the wings of the dawn, if I settle on the far side of the sea, even there your hand will guide me, your right hand will hold me fast.

If I say, 'Surely the darkness will hide me and the light become night around me,' even the darkness will not be dark to you; the night will shine like the day, for darkness is as light to you.

For you created my inmost being; you knit me together in my mother's womb. I praise you because I am fearfully and wonderfully made; your works are wonderful, I know that full well. My frame was not hidden from you when I was made in the secret place. When I was woven together in the depths of the earth, your eyes saw my unformed body. All the days ordained for me were written in your book before one of them came to be.

How precious to me are your thoughts, O God! How vast is the sum of them! Were I to count them, they would outnumber the grains of sand. When I awake I am still with you.
Psalm 149:1-18

What a picture of our Creator! It almost matches the New Testament picture in Romans 11:33-36:

Oh, the depths of the riches of the wisdom and knowledge of God! How unsearchable are his judgments, and his paths beyond tracing out! Who has known the mind of the Lord? Or who has been his counsellor? Who has ever given to God, that

God should repay him? For from him and through him and to him are all things.

Should we not take very seriously the words: "for from him and through him and to him are all things?" Do they not tell us something about God's creative and sustaining work?

Through Isaiah the same infinite One speaks to us all:

> To whom will you compare me? Or who is my equal? says the Holy One. Lift up your eyes and look to the heavens: who created all these? He who brings out the starry host one by one, and calls them each by name. Because of his great power and mighty strength, not one of them is missing.
> 40: 25-26

Every day we make a hundred decisions without adequate knowledge. There is a sense in which we are all living and moving in the dark. "We walk by faith and not by sight" (2 Cor. 5:7). But it is our privilege to interpret the unknown by the known. All other knowledge apart from the knowledge of God is only chaff. We need chaff, but how much more do we need the divine wheat? Loren Wilkinson has written some excellent things on our topic. Note the following:

> The upholding energies of the Creator are necessary *at every instant* for each thing to be. There is no question of God intervening in such a creation, because each thing depends for its very existence on God. If God were not in some way upholding the creature's existence, the creature would cease to exist. ... As one orthodox theologian, Philaret of Moscow, puts it: 'All creatures are balanced upon the creative word of God, as if upon a bridge of diamond, above them is the abyss of divine infinitude, below them that of their own nothingness.'
> Chapter: "Does Methodological Naturalism Lead to Metaphysical Naturalism?", in Phillip E. Johnson and Denis O. Lamoureux (eds.), *Darwinism Defeated? The Johnson-Lamoureux Debate on Biological Origins,* Vancouver, BC, 1999, page 173 (citing *Metropolitan Philaret of Moscow,* cited in Kallistos Ware, *The Orthodox Way,* page 57, n3)

Then Wilkinson gives us more from Kallistos Ware:

> As the fruit of God's free will and free love, the world is not necessary and not self-sufficient, but *contingent* and *dependant*. As created things we can never be just ourselves alone. God is the core of our being, or we cease to exist. At every moment we depend for our existence upon the loving will of God. Existence is always a *gift* from God.
> *Ibid.*, page 57

And once more:

> As creator, then, God is always at the heart of each thing, maintaining it in being. On the level of scientific inquiry, we discern certain processes or sequences of cause and effect. On the level of spiritual vision, which does not contradict science but looks beyond it, we discern everywhere the creative energies of God, upholding all that is, forming the inmost essence of all things. But God is not to be identified with the world. ... God is in all things yet also *beyond and above* all things.
> *Ibid.*, page 58

"Work out your own salvation with fear and trembling, for it is God who works in you to will and to act according to his good purpose" (Phil 2:12-13). Thus it is also with all of divine activity in all of nature and life. Jesus is very emphatic that God's activity is continuous. See John 5:17.

So my view of progressive creation may not be identical with that of others who use the term. By it I signify my belief that not chance but God is behind all life in all its various stages. What scientists described as the "abrupt" appearance of new kinds is really the willing and creative power of God. This I believe is the clear teaching of Scripture. "You are worthy, our Lord and God. To receive glory and honor and power, for you created all things, and *by your will they were created and have their being*" (Rev. 4:11).

May I summarize the steps leading to this conclusion:

1.   The dissatisfaction of a multitude of scientists, especially biologists and paleoanthropologists, with Darwinism and neo-Darwinism has been greatly strengthened by recent research.

2.   Gould's declaration that Darwinism is "effectively dead" has found abundant supporting evidence among paleontologists around the world.

3.   In the last half century Darwinian gradualism has been disproved by the experience of all who investigate the geologic column.

4.   The term most often used about the appearance of new species is "abrupt." See Bird's first volume for many examples.

5.   Chance could not produce a thimble, let alone beings whose brains have 10^{15} connections and a liver which performs 500 functions, not to speak of the eye and the ear, and a thousand other physical marvels.

6.   Genesis 12:2,3; Deuteronomy 18:15-19; Psalm 22; Isaiah 52:13—53:12; Daniel 9:24-27; Micah 5:2; Matthew 24:35; Acts 1:8; John 8:12; John 3:16; Romans 3:19-28; 4:8; 5:1, and the testimony of the four Gospels to the Son of God incarnate who was crucified but rose again (seen by 500 witnesses at one time—1 Corinthians 15:6) give abundant evidence for the honest searcher that there is a supernatural Deity who is behind both Scripture and Nature.

7.   The experience of millions of believing Christians over 2,000 years has demonstrated the reality of the Creator's special care over those committed to him, and his general providence over all of life.

8.   Time is short. Choices are determined chiefly by our *Weltanschaung*—our beliefs about the origin and nature of this planet and life.

9.   If chance is at the heart of existence, nothing has value, our brains cannot be trusted, and our existence is meaningless. "Let us eat and drink, and be merry, for tomorrow we die." But if a heart of love, a hand of power, and a mind of infinite knowledge is at the heart of the universe, then life can be not only worth living, but a

glorious privilege and joy unspeakable. The believer has everything to gain and nothing to lose, but the unbeliever has everything to lose and nothing to gain.

Chapter Twenty-six Summary:

Progressive Creationism solves the problems of geology, archaeology, and accepted science. It teaches that God is the author of all life and that he has willed into existence successive kinds and ultimately our first parents. A quote from Bernard Ramm is helpful:

> Over the millions of years of geologic history the earth is prepared for man's dwelling. ... The vast forests grew and decayed for his coal, that coal might appear a natural product and not an artificial insertion in Nature. The millions of sea life were born and perished for his oil. The surface of the earth was weathered for his forests and valleys. From time to time, the great creative acts *de novo* took place. The complexity of animal forms increased. Finally, when every river had cut its intended course, when every mountain was in its purposed place, when every animal was on the earth according to blueprint, then he whom all creation anticipated is made, MAN, in whom alone is the breath of God.
> *The Christian View of Science and Scripture,* pages 227-228

CHAPTER 27

The First Adam's Descendants

WHAT SORT OF men and women were the ancient humans? We know very little about their character, or even who were our first ancestors. The Neanderthals mysteriously become extinct and their more gifted successors dominated earth. Ian Tattersall, probably the paleontologist who knows most about these ancestors of ours, pictures their probable end:

> We will never know for certain what happened. All we can say with assurance is that in the end, the moderns won out. It may be that despite their species difference, the Neanderthals and moderns were similar enough to interbreed—or perhaps more likely, the urge to ravish. It's vanishingly unlikely, however, that peaceful assimilation was an overall option, with groups of the two kinds of humans exchanging members when they met and going their separate ways, or joining forces. More likely, perhaps, if intermixing is to be considered at all, is a scenario of well-equipped and cunning *Homo sapiens* descending on Neanderthal groups, killing the males—through strategy and guile, certainly not through strength—and abducting the females. Yet it's highly improbable that visible offspring could have been produced by the resulting unions. Neanderthal females would hardly have been of much reproductive value to the invaders.
>
> Whatever the details, in view of the ways that invading *Homo sapiens* have tended to treat resident members of their own as well as other species throughout recorded history, encounters between *Homo neanderthalensis* and *Homo sapiens* probably were not often happy ones. ... but it is profoundly misleading to see them (the Neanderthals) simply as an inferior version of ourselves.
> *The Last Neanderthal*, pages 202-203

Whether this is the correct or whole story of the demise of the Neanderthals we do not know. Let us not be troubled by that. Recent research suggests that Neanderthals and *Homo Sapiens* were contemporaries for many thousands of years. As Edison told us long ago, we know less than one percent about anything. You cannot look around indoors or outdoors without being confronted by mysteries. One hundred times a day we all make decisions with very inadequate evidence. There is no avoiding the fork in the road.

Perhaps the most distinguishing mark of sin is its power to lead men to make war upon their brothers. All of history is a history of war. The further a man gets from his heavenly Father the further he gets from his brother. It is akin to the spokes of a wheel, which get closer as they near the hub and further from each other as they leave the hub. Wherever there is evidence of man killing man we have evidence of the Fall, the rebellion of our first parents. This gives weight to Tattersall's conclusions about the Neanderthals, but even more does it give weight to the truth revealed by the murderer Cain, "Am I my brother's keeper?" Yes, Cain, you were, and we are. Such is the depth of the statement in Genesis 4.

At first we may feel disconcerted by the idea that the Bible could omit so much of human history. Surely it would be good to know more about the Neanderthals and the Cro-Magnons. We forget so easily that early populations were considerably less than a fragment of one percent of today's population.

Have we fully understood the way in which Christ concentrated the history of many centuries into a story of just nine verses? See Matthew 21:33-41. Please consider: how much of the spectrum of knowledge did the Living Word Christ Jesus unveil when he came? Were not his words narrowly restricted to what was moral and theological? He could have discoursed on a million topics but he chose just a few. Paul does the same in his inspired Epistles. God is very practical; he does not load us down with knowledge that is not pertinent to our way of life. The Bible is a very practical book. Consider the bewilderment the first readers of Genesis would have experienced if the whole story of ancient history had then been told them. It was much better to use well-known memories passed down orally about real people and real events and shape them so as to help believers in all their decision-making and their worship of the one true God.

Wherein does progressive creation (which teaches the reality of Adam and the Fall) differ from theistic evolution? First let us consider theistic evolution itself. It is a great mistake to speak slightingly of those committed to this faith. Many great Christians of the nineteenth century and since have been theistic evolutionists. Henry Drummond (author of *The Greatest Thing in the World),* Charles Kingsley, James Orr, Benjamin Warfield, and in recent times, John Polkinghorne, Arthur Peacocke, John Stott, and J. I. Packer, etc. The list is endless. We must not forget our brothers and sisters in the Roman Catholic faith. Theistic evolution has been held in that portion of the Christian community from the very beginning of the evolution controversy. Probably the best-known book on the topic today is *Creation or Evolution* by Denis Alexander, but it is not one I recommend.

The main criticism by some concerning theistic evolution is that it is rather "woolly" about the facticity of Adam, Eve, and the Fall. This does not fit all theistic evolutionists. For instance, it does not fit John Stott. In view of Luke 3, Romans 5, 1 Corinthians 15, and the Book of Jude it is very difficult to deny the reality of Adam. "In Adam all die, in Christ all are made alive" (1 Cor. 15:22). There is a sense in which the whole Bible rests on the historicity of the Fall recorded in Genesis 3. If there was no Fall there is no need of redemption and, therefore, no need of Christ and his Cross. To deny the Fall is to ignore and contradict the hourly constant experience of every person who has ever lived. And it fails to explain the agonized cry of the best man in history (after Christ): "O wretched man that I am!" (Romans 7:24).

The Genesis picture of beginnings is one that begins at a high and happy point but then progressively deteriorates all the way to the account of The Tower of Babel. With theistic evolution the direction is in reverse. With it the trend is always upwards. This is not what Moses says.

Belief in progressive creation enables us to acknowledge the assured facts about both inspired records of Scripture and the facts of science. We know that this world is four and a half billion years old. We know that God first created single-celled creatures and then progressively brought on the scene more complex forms of life and finally man. We know that Genesis is inspired but also that it is God's way of speaking, not ours. We know that Genesis 1-11 reflects many of the current myths of Israel's polytheistic neighbours and protests against them, transforming them. God chose to envelop his theological truth in parabolic form as Christ did when ministering to men.

Genesis by its revelation of God and truth is self-authenticating to the sincere reader. Its types and prophecies of the coming Savior further authenticate it.

We know that the well-intentioned efforts of Creationists to prove a young earth and a universal flood have failed. The view of earth's history so offered is false. Ours is the duty of acknowledging as truth all that God has made clear in both Scripture and nature. If our view of one contradicts our interpretation of the other we have erred and must look again. They agree. The geologic column is a fact that no one can deny and it proves beyond all doubt the great age of the earth, and the progressive unfolding of life's forms with man at the summit. Death is implicit in the record—otherwise there would have been overcrowding and subsequent recurrent universal starvation. When Scripture in Romans 5 says that death entered our race with Adam, it is referring to human death. No one could even walk among Eden's bowers without inflicting death on microscopic forms of life, and the daily diet meant death to plants and fruit. Did not the elephant's descending feet wreak havoc among the minute lives in the dust?

A child or an ignorant man without education can grasp the lessons of Genesis. It is not necessary that they understand science. But if that child and man ultimately must encounter unbelievers they will need to know more than they presently do. And that knowledge is readily available. God does all things well, and both nature and Scripture testify of his love and power and wisdom. Alleluia! Darwin famously expressed his certainty that every point he had made would be debated with attempts of refutation. He was right. May I say the same as regards this small venture? But remember this: Life is brief, our attention span is limited, and so is our degree of intelligence, but truth is infinite. It is not linear but polygonal. We are forced to decide all important issues according to the weight of evidence. As regards our present discussions, I believe the weight of evidence is abundant and overflowing for those who really want to know.

Despite post-modernism and the buffoonery of some neo-atheists like Richard Dawkins, Christians have every reason to be encouraged by many of the developments in our day. Dr. C. E. M. Joad began a pilgrimage of many thinkers back to faith. Dr. Antony Flew is the most recent and the most well known. But there are others who once jeered at the Christian gospel. A. N. Wilson, well known across the intellectual world, once surrendered Christianity and spent years mocking, yet now he has returned home. In an interview with the *New Statesman* he confessed that atheists "were missing out on some very basic experiences of life." After listening to Bach and re-reading religious authors he acknowledged that their worldview or "perception of life was deeper, wiser, and more rounded than my own."

Perhaps before this chapter is closed a brief summary of the impact of Darwinism is appropriate. From 1870 to 1914 there was one prolonged cry for blood. The worst wars of extermination known to history took place after the publication of *The Origin of Species*. Perhaps the most terrible prolonged cataclysm was the slaughter in the Belgian Congo in the early years of last century. Millions of deaths were perpetrated in the Belgian Congo by whites who were certain of their racial superiority and the need to win in the struggle for existence.

Darwinism had tremendous influence on Marxism. Karl Marx probably read the *Origin* in 1860 and immediately offered to dedicate *Das Kapital* to Darwin. But for social reasons the offer was refused. Marx exclaimed with much joy, "Now I have a basis in science for the class struggle throughout all of history." Mussolini took hold of Darwin's primary ideas, and he repeatedly used Darwinian catchwords in his perorations. Adoph Hitler apparently read the *Origin* in his youth, for all of his subsequent speeches and *Mein Kampf* resonate with

Darwinian phrases. His determination to destroy the Jewish race sprang from his conviction that the supremacy of the German people was an evolutionary ideal. Therefore, there must be no intermarriage between Germans and people of lower stock. On the same grounds he began to destroy the inmates of asylums and other institutions. Long before Hitler and Mussolini, their favourite philosopher, Friedrich Nietzsche, had swallowed Darwinism totally. It permeates his brilliantly written, but fallacious philosophy, which became the seedbed for noxious political plants in the following decades.

The greatest impact in terms of individuals fell upon the youth. Soon it was apparent that this was a postmodern generation permeated by relativism, pluralism, and naturalism. For the youth this ideological explosion wrought a deep-seated anger at the meaningless of their existence. Violence, unbridled lust, and an ever-increasing surge towards suicide resulted. Today in many countries, particularly in Muslim lands, the fear of governments has to do with their youth generation, which is ever ready to explode in violence. And inasmuch as the chief proportion of Muslim people is the youth generation this is a danger indeed.

To remove God from human life, as has often been pointed out, is to remove sanctity and to wipe one's feet on the doormat of Auschwitz. If there is no God, neither is there man (only a biological blob). There is no meaning, no hope, no forgiveness, no eternal life, but also no right and wrong and no love. Therefore the brakes against the cataclysmic outpouring of violence and brutality are removed. Today technology has made available to people everywhere, but especially to the young, the worst elements of our civilization. The dregs of Hollywood, physical and sexual violence, pornography, etc., are seeping into even pre-juvenile minds. With the proliferation of technology and gadgets such as iPhones and iPads, the gates are thrown open for children to view and develop a taste for all forms of evil. Even young pre-teen children may be belittled and bullied by their peers to force them to participate in the same things that porn stars would peruse. Thus the sexual barriers are eviscerated, bringing the inevitable consequences of rape, venereal diseases, partner violence, unwanted pregnancies and so on. This is just one example of the rapid proliferation of evil in a world where many have thrown out God.[1]

When one reviews the literature covering the decades from 1860 to our own age, one notices the very strange reluctance to say much about the evolutionary causes of our modern chaos. This is because writers are afraid to be classified as fundamentalist Christians. But the greatest among them, such as Gertrude Himmelfarb, have no such hesitation. The facts do indeed speak for themselves.

If, in the midst of arcane discussion, I have failed to make first things first I apologize to you. Genesis, as with the rest of Scripture, is primarily about the gospel. May I therefore summarize what I believe that gospel to be?

Not only passages like Genesis 12:2,3, Isaiah 52-53, Psalm 22, and Matthew 24:35 prove the supernatural origin of Scripture, but the story of Calvary repeated four times because of its preeminent importance touches not only our heads but melts our hearts. Never forget this: *No Jew could ever have invented the story of a crucified Messiah!* This is the unique teaching of a God so in love with his rebel creatures that he would suffer untold insult and pain on their behalf and in their place! This is beyond human invention. The Bible is such a book that men would not write if they could and could not if they would.

The gospel is built around this story: 2 Cor 5:14: "If one died for all, then all died." Christ was not only our substitute, but also our representative. If we believe the gospel we are counted as having done what he did. We also died on Calvary (in our representative) and paid then for all our sins—past, present, and future. Now, whosoever will may come, for all manner of sin and blasphemy can be forgiven to men, and he that comes, God will in no wise cast out.

---

1   Cambridge geologist, Professor Adam Sedgwick, labeled the *Origin* as a dish of rank materialism, cleverly cooked and served up merely to make us independent of a Creator. He prophesied that if Darwin's teachings were accepted, humanity would suffer a damage that might brutalize it and sink the human race into a lower grade of degradation than any into which it has fallen since its written records of its history. Carlyle agreed and stigmatized Darwin as a man of only mediocre intelligence. See Robert E. D. Clark, *Darwin: Before and After*, page 96 for the Sedgewick quotation and much more.

Our justification (being counted or reckoned righteous before God) is not only for the first moment of accepting his gospel offer. It is over us through all our days and in all our ways. For we are saved by faith alone, though the faith that saves is never alone. We are saved not by faith plus works, but by a faith that works. Every moment the believer is accepted in the Beloved and complete in him, despite a million stumblings. God forgives us to seventy times seven and then stops counting, even if you owe heaven 14 million dollars (Matthew 18). The righteousness of justification is 100 percent, but it is an accounted righteousness, not a making righteous. So our righteousness is in heaven, in our Savior. The righteousness of sanctification (the Christian growth in Christ-likeness) is never 100 percent, but it is within us through the working of the Holy Spirit. The righteousness of glorification at the resurrection will be a righteousness that is both 100 percent and within us forever and ever.

Only God and heaven can be had for the asking. You don't have to be good to be saved, but you must be saved to be good. Here is a melody that lifts us above life's sorrows and problems and girds us with strength to fight the fight of faith. Believe, and you will see the glory of God. Go forward, is not the whole land before you, the land flowing with milk and honey? Heaven and all its gifts are yours for the taking. Christ by faith is *your* Christ and God *your* God. What more could any one want than what the gospel offers to every man and woman today? Remember, its not *who* you are, but *whose*. And if you have a problem about your personal salvation remember that God has promised to save all who *call* upon him. See Romans 10:13. For all other problems of an intellectual nature you have the wise counsel of our Lord: "What is that to thee, follow thou me" (John 21:22).

May I share with you the wonderful words of R. W. Dale?

> Tell men that, while they inherit by their birth the infirmities and sins of the race, they also inherit by their birth the salvation, which Christ has achieved for all mankind. Tell them that they live, not in a lost world, but in a redeemed world; a world lost by its revolt against God and its alienation from the life of God, but redeemed in the blood of Christ, and with power in Christ, and in the Spirit of Christ, which render all

righteousness possible. Tell men—all men—that they were created in Christ, and that when they discover and accept their true relation to Him, they will live under new heavens and in a new earth, and will know the greatness of the sons of God. Tell them that they are blessed with every spiritual blessing in Christ; that God chose them in Him before the foundation of the world, that they should be holy and without blemish before Him in love; charge them not to defeat this purpose of Divine grace, but to work out their salvation with fear and trembling, and so to make their calling and election sure. See to it that through God's grace you know for yourselves that, by the merits of Christ, your sins are forgiven, and that you are indeed, and of a truth, the children of God, that your testimony to the Christian redemption may not rest on tradition, but on your own personal experience.
Centenary Sermons and Addresses, pages 89-90

Read Romans 8:28-39 every day and sing from overflowing and fearless hearts and sane minds. Remember, "ultimately the believer has no questions, and ultimately the atheist has no answers."

CHAPTER TWENTY-SEVEN SUMMARY:

There really were Neanderthals and Cro-Magnon people of pre-history. They are not inventions. The evidence of their existence is overwhelming and denied by no paleontologist. What happened to the Neanderthals is an insistent question. But the one fact to be certain about is the Christian gospel.

RECOMMENDED READING

Bird, Wm. R. *The Origin of Species Revisited,* Volume 1, Nashville, TN, Thomas Nelson, 1991.

Blocher, Henri. *In the Beginning.* Nottingham, UK: Intervarsity Press, 1994.

Croft, L.R. *How Life Began,* El Cajon, CA, Evangelical Press, 1998.

Denton, Michael *Evolution: A Theory in Crisis,* Chicago, IL, Adler & Adler, 2002.

Denton, Michael *Nature's Destiny : How the Laws of Biology Reveal Purpose in the Universe,* New York, N.Y., Simon & Schuster, 2002.

Flew, Antony *There is a God,* New York, NY, HarperCollins, 2007. Strobel, Lee *The Case for a Creator,* Grand Rapids, MI, 2004.

Hayward, Alan *Creation and Evolution,* Eugene, OR, Wipf & Stock, 2005.

Himmelfarb, Gertrude *Darwin and the Darwinian Revolution,* New York, NY, Ivan R. Dee, 1996, reprint.

Hugh Ross, *The Fingerprint of God,* New Kensington, PA, Whitaker House, 2000.

Simmons, Geoffrey *What Darwin Didn't Know,* Eugene, OR, Harvest House, 2004.

Strobel, Lee *The Case for a Creator,* Grand Rapids, MI, 2004.

Ward, Rowland S. *Foundations in Genesis,* Melbourne, VIC, New Melbourne Press, 1998.

Wenham, Gordon J. *Word Biblical Commentary, Genesis 1-15,* Waco, TX, Word Press, 1991.

OUR PRESENT CRISIS AND A SIMPLE SOLUTION

THE ADVENTIST CHURCH is in danger of being torn apart. And the first to leave will be the best educated. The cause is well known—the controversy over the first chapter of the Bible. Does the chapter suggest a young earth or an old one? Must we believe in a globe between six and ten thousand years old, or can we in good conscience understand these opening words of Scripture as applying to a very old creation?

Most of our science teachers in our colleges and universities believe in a very old earth and for excellent reasons that are readily available to anyone who reads.

Many modern exegetes tell us that an appropriate translation for Genesis 1:1 states, "in the beginning God created the universe." See, for example, the commentaries by Victor P. Hamilton and Gordon Wenham—scholars acknowledged around the world as first class.

The *Word Biblical Commentary* on Genesis 1-15 was published in 1987. We quote it:

> 'The heaven and the earth.' It is characteristic of many languages to describe 'the totality of something in terms of its extremes, e.g., 'good and bad,' 'big and little,' etc. Here we have an example of this usage to define the universe (cf. J. Krasovec, *Der Meris-mus im Biblisch-Hebräischen and Nordwestsemitischen*, BibOr 33 [Rome: Biblical Institute Press, 1977], pages 16-25

> On its own *shamayim*[1] means 'sky' or 'heaven,' i.e., the abode of God, while *erets* denotes the 'earth, world,' which is man's house. But in the OT, as well as in Egyptian, Akkadian, and

---

1   The English equivalent has been used to replace the Hebrew for *shamayim* and *erets* here.

Ugaritic, 'heaven and earth' may also be used to denote the universe. (M. Ottosson, *TDOT* 1:389-91; Stadelmann, *Hebrew Conception of the World, 1-2; Gen. 14:19,22; 24:3; Isa. 66:1; Ps. 89:12)* ...

Genesis 1:1 could therefore be translated, 'In the beginning God created everything.' Commentators often insist that the phrase 'heaven and earth' denotes the completely ordered cosmos. page 15 (*Word Biblical Commentary* on Genesis 1-15)

A more popular work says the same thing essentially:

Old Testament Hebrew had no word for 'universe' so it used 'the heavens and the earth' instead. That phrase is one of the biblical ways of saying 'all things' (Eccles. 11:5; Is. 44:24; Jer. 10:16; John 1:3) since everything that exists is either on earth or in the heavens (broadly conceived.)
Ronald Youngblood, *The Book of Genesis*, 2nd edn, page 23

But no Adventist is dependent upon the literary skills of scholarship to prove this point. The Bible does it for us and in just the right place. See Genesis 2:1: "Thus the heavens and the earth were finished and all the host of them" (KJV). Or, in the New International Version: "Thus the heavens and the earth were completed in all their vast array."

The word translated "host" or "vast array" is used in Scripture for an army (Gen. 21:22); the stars (Deut. 4:19) or angels (1 Kings 22:19). Practically all commentators understand the term here to signify the stars of heaven. This summary verse at the close of the creation story is looking back on all that God has done including the making of the sun, moon, and stars referred to on the fourth day.

The clincher, of course, is Genesis 1:16 (NIV):

God made two great lights—the greater light to govern the day and the lesser light to govern the night. He also made the stars.

The Hebrew is quite clear: the making of the stars was part of the same process that led to the sun and moon. The common theory that "make" here means "reveal" will not stand. The Hebrew for "appear" occurs in Genesis 1:9 and it is not the same as the Hebrew of verse 16. There is no escaping the fact that Genesis says God created the heavenly bodies on the fourth day. This implies that the earth was made before the rest of the universe—only understandable if history and science were the last things in the mind of the inspiring Spirit.

There is nothing new in the present contentions. The *Pulpit Commentary* was published over a century ago. We quote from its discussion of Genesis 1:1:

> *The heavens and the earth (i.e. mundus universus*—Gesenius, Kalisch, etc.) Cf. ch 2:1; 14:19,22; Ps. 115:15; Jer. 23:24. The earth and the heavens always mean the terrestrial globe with its aerial firmament. Cf. 2:4; Ps. 148:13; Zech. 5:9). The earth here alluded to is manifestly not the dry land (ver. 10), which was not separated from the waters till the third day, but the entire mass of which our planet is composed, including the superincumbent atmosphere, which was not uplifted from the chaotic deep till the second day. The heavens are the rest of the universe. Vol. 1, page 3

Therefore, the teaching of Genesis 1 is crystal clear—it is referring to the making of the entire universe. It is this fact that guarantees that the week under review is a parabolic one, and that primeval creation dates back long, long eras ago. It is difficult to imagine that some people still think that the universe is 6,000 years old, and any denomination that does so will never win educated people.

I venture to quote my recent book *Genesis Versus Darwinism; The Demise of Darwin's Theory of Evolution:*

> Young people who frequently have had little acquaintance with literature tend to take everything they read literally. But the Bible contains many types of literature—poetry, law, history, apocalyptic, prophecy, doctrinal statements, and so on. Also the Bible is full of figures of speech and symbols. For example, the serpent in Genesis chapter 3 is interpreted in Revelation 12 as Satan, and the four Gospels set forth the Cross as the true Tree

of life and Tree of knowledge. The forecast of the end of the
world (Revelation) is full of symbols. What about the account
of the beginning of the world? When time and eternity meet,
pictures are inevitable.

No one takes literally all the saying of Christ. 'If your eye offend
you pluck it out, and if your hand offend you cut it off,' is but
one instance. Christ's speech is full of metaphors. He speaks
of moving mountains, of people who swallow camels. He tells
us that we must eat his flesh and drink his blood. John 10:6
states that Christ spoke in allegories (original). Most people
in churches still have both eyes and both hands! When Christ
declares himself to be the Door, the Vine, the Bread of Life, for
example, we recognize that he is using symbols. The whole book
of Revelation is a series of pictures, for one picture is better than
10,000 words. In real life there are no beasts with seven heads
and ten horns, nor will Christ literally appear on an Arabian
steed with a sword protruding from his mouth, despite the portrayal in Revelation chapters 13, 17, and 19.

One-third of Christ's teachings are in the form of parables,
and there are inspired parables in the Old Testament as well.
Parables teach the truth by pictures and stories, not by literal
arguments (the kingdom of God is LIKE ...). Luke 16: 19-31
is not taken literally by those comprehending the text. The Bible
nowhere teaches a present fiery hell (especially not in Hades,
verse 23, which means the grave), or that heaven and such a hell
are in conversational distance.
Desmond Ford, *Genesis Versus Darwinism*, p. xii

The early chapters of Genesis contain many symbols or metaphors.
God himself is anthropomorphically pictured as breathing (Genesis
2:7), speaking (Genesis 1) doing surgical work (Genesis 2: 21,22),
gardening (Genesis 2:8ff) and tailoring (Genesis 3:21). He declares
that the serpent henceforth will eat dust. Nobody literalizes that.

Consider how Exodus 31:17 tell us that God was "refreshed" by his
Sabbath rest. But elsewhere Scripture assures us that the Lord God
"faints not, neither is weary." So the NIV translates the Hebrew into

a more acceptable term. But Christ in John 5 assures us that God has never stopped working. See verse 17, which assures us that God is ALWAYS toiling.

Those who wish to take everything in the Bible literally will have an untold number of difficulties. Take 1 Corinthians 7:1, which says a man should not touch a woman. Yet the same Paul believes in marriage as honourable. If you take "all things are yours" literally, you will end up in jail. As Ellen White has told us God as a writer is not represented in Scripture. His chosen words gifted to us are human words and everything human is imperfect. And yet the Bible IS perfect—perfect for its purpose.

Siegfried Horn, the scholar who had most to do with the chronology of the *SDA Bible Commentary* and *SDA Dictionary*, always refused to offer any certain dates prior to the call of Abraham. Dr Horn's diary makes it clear that he rejected all efforts to prove a young earth. We would do well to follow his example.

Many of our problems arise from inadequate exegesis of Genesis. We have never made it clear to our people that the word for Adam in Genesis chapters 1-3 is customarily prefaced by the Hebrew article "ha," making it clear that in these chapters there is no personal name, only a reference to generic man.

The words of Derek Kidner and Charles Foster are helpful:

> If Genesis is abbreviating a long history, the sheer vastness of the ages it spans is not so sharp a problem as the fact that almost the whole of the immensity lies, for the paleontologist, between the first man and the first farmer—that is, between Adam and Cain, *or even between Adam inside and outside Eden.*
> Derek Kidner, *Genesis,* page 27

Kidner's problem is solved when we understand that a personal Adam with that name only appears in Genesis 4 many ages after the pristine beauties of Genesis 2. Thus Genesis 1 and 2 describe a time eons before the development of cities, musicians, and tradespeople as featured in Genesis 4. Genesis 4 belongs to approximately 10,000

B.C., but the preceding chapters belong to the ages (deep time). Adam in Genesis 1 is not the same Adam as in Genesis 4.

Here now is Foster:

> The formulation used to denote Adam throughout the first three chapters of Genesis is *Ha Adam*. But that, in Hebrew, is not a personal name at all. It simply means 'the human.' Adam is not used as a given name, to denote a particular individual, until chapter 4.
> *The Selfless Gene*, page 129

There is no need to invoke theistic evolution. Genesis 2:7 is not saying that God took an advanced hominid and breathed a human personality into him. Theistic evolution always has the early things getting better and better, but the Genesis story is the reverse. The New Testament knows nothing of theistic evolution and always uses Adam as a real person, the father of humanity.

Seventh-day Adventists are evangelicals but not fundamentalists. The difference chiefly consists in this, that like the fathers of the Reformation and the originators of Methodism we take scholarship seriously. Similarly, we acknowledge true science as one of God's good gifts. How thankful we are for it when requiring surgery! Think of the agonizing surgeries done before the days of chloroform!

On the other hand there is no basis for worshiping science. It is carried out by imperfect humans, and its erroneous theories over the decades have been innumerable. For example see the recent book by E. O. Wilson, *The Meaning of Human Existence*, which documents how in our times hundreds of scientists have taken the wrong path and erred in their own field (see pages 66-75).

It is almost humorous when we read of the world famous evolutionary biologist Wilson endorsing a new theory, then recanting, and then enduring rebuke from 137 fellow scientists (including Richard Dawkins), who were themselves in error. It would make a great movie. God has two books—Scripture and nature—and we would do well to constantly study both books. But if we so interpret them as to

161

make them conflict, we will have erred regarding one or the other. Then is the time to humbly re-examine until disagreement ceases.

Let us, therefore, not only be cautious about science, but also about our own traditions.

Genesis 1-11: A Different Genre— Let's Tell the Truth

ADVENTISTS HAVE LONG prided themselves as being "the people of the book." Has not Ellen White insisted in the beginning and near the end of her book, *The Great Controversy*, pages 9 and 595, that the Bible and the Bible only is the source of religious truth? But could it be that our pride is misplaced and that it is only a form of ignorant thoughtlessness?

In Adventist circles controversies regarding Genesis are not about chapters 12–50 but the first eleven chapters. Our disagreements with old-earthers and evolutionists stem from our interpretation of these initial chapters of the Bible's opening book. For example, chapters 6–8 are about the Flood and Noah, and for over 100 years Adventists have accepted the comments of Ellen G. White regarding the nature of that Flood. We have taught by voice and pen that the geologic column with its fossils is the evidence and result of the worldwide deluge.

Here, of course, we clash with almost all paleontologists and geologists who insist that the column could not have been born in the catastrophe of a single year but is the result of long ages. The evidence for this is impossible to deny—are not the earliest fossils chiefly of single-celled variety or algae etc., followed by strata with increasingly complex forms of ancient life? There are no human skeletons partway through the column. There is no mixture of human and animal fossils suggesting a giant catastrophe that mixed together all living things. There is just no evidence for that. The various geologic strata are progressively aged. (There are now about fifty methods of dating the earth and its contents, and while some may squabble about a few of these methods it is not possible to reject the combined testimony of the rest.) The admitted absence of transitional forms indicates progressive creation, not evolution.

Only in the third world are Adventists winning significant numbers of people. Elsewhere our evangelistic efforts are barren. Very few educated people attend any meetings advertised by SDAs. And so long as we insist on advocating hoary traditions long ago exploded we will never reach the ear of people of intelligence and culture.

Let me illustrate our impact (or lack of such) upon the learned. The book, *The Selfless Gene,* by Charles Foster is a deliberate slight upon Richard Dawkins' *The Selfish Gene.* Foster has no love for Dawkins and goes out of his way to say why—even taking a whole book to do it.

Well, we agree with Foster there. We too, agree with those who consider Dawkins a scientific journalist of the fundamentalist variety. But now let us discuss more important things. Foster's book says many good things despite his agreement with evolution, but he has no love for Adventism.

On page xiv of his preface Foster writes:

> In his 1860 debate with Huxley, Wilberforce tried to parody Darwinism into extinction. He famously failed. Since then, Christianity and Darwinism coexisted pretty happily—although with little real conversation—until the relatively recent rise of creationism, a movement that sprang fully deformed from the loins of Seventh-day Adventism.

Then on page 23 we read:

> The roots of modern creationism go further back. Its pedigree is soundly Seventh-Day Adventist. The founder of Seventh-day Adventism, Ellen G. White, claimed to have been shown by God in a vision in 1864 that he had created the world in six twenty-four hour days, and that the fossils were all artifacts of the Noahic flood. These ideas were promulgated by George McCready Price in his *New Geology* (1923), and taken up, popularized and transmuted into the Young Earthers' canon by Henry Morris.

Now the first thing you noticed about that statement was that Foster doesn't know everything—he doesn't even know the capitalization for Seventh-day Adventists. The second thing to note is this: by creationists he means chiefly those who are committed to a young earth of between six and ten thousand years. That does not embrace all Seventh-day Adventists.

But the main thing we should notice is that here we have a representation of the way many intelligent people view Adventists. Of course, we can keep our sailing ship afloat moving between third-world ports and continue to shrink as regards educated first-world parishioners. Or, we can follow the counsel of a fallible but wise pioneer who advised us to give up long cherished views if further information proved them to be wrong.

You may have noticed that the original *SDA Bible Commentary* reflected George McCready Price in the relevant areas of Genesis, but the more recent edition does not. Of course, we still cling to the idea that the fossils came only from the Flood, but we have learned that Price was just plain wrong in many things that he wrote—godly and intelligent man though he undoubtedly was.

We live now in the twenty-first century, not the nineteenth. Much has been learned and proved over that period, and because of the computer age and the Internet it is difficult to ward off what seem to be bombshells on the "remnant." It is now undeniable that Ellen White and the early Adventist church in general believed in a "shut door," excluding the rest of the world from salvation. We have learned that the "Dark Day" mentioned in *The Great Controversy* came from forest fires, and that the meteoric showers of 1833 were the Leonids that arrive every 33 years. We no longer teach that Turkey is coming to its end with no one to help her—a prelude to Christ's return. We no longer teach that Daniel 12:4 has to do with scientific knowledge. Even the famous Armageddon battle in God's ancient land has lost its popularity among scholars in the fields of exegesis and eschatology. The list is very long. These offer but a sample.

Our own scientists in our colleges and universities do not teach the things advocated by George McCready Price. Most of them do not believe that Noah's Flood caused the millions of fossils since excavated from the column. They consent, for the most part, that our world is four-and-a-half billion years old. Many other Adventists who give themselves to reading agree with the typical scientific view.

I well remember a few years ago attending a lecture by Ken Ham of *Answers in Genesis*. In the Question Period I asked him if he could name a single geologist respected by his peers who agreed with the stance taken in *The Genesis Flood* by Whitcomb and Morris (the bible of fundamentalist young-earthers). He did not answer my question, but moved on to another topic for obvious reasons. Whitcomb and Morris could not find any support from geologists for their theories about the Flood of Noah and the geologic column, which had been borrowed from Price.

Yet, it is clear that Genesis IS talking about a worldwide flood. There is no need for a giant vessel to succour animals and people if the coming flood could be avoided by migration. For well over 2,000 years commentators on Genesis have been agreed that the Flood of Genesis chapters 6 to 8 was worldwide. How could it be otherwise when we are told that the water covered the highest mountains by fifteen cubits?

Strangely, the solution to this problem does not seem to have occurred to most Fundamentalist Christians. It is quite simple. Consider how the contents of Genesis 1–11 are beyond all human experience and thus are often described as mega history. We have not talked with God as did Adam and Eve, and we have not known a pristine Eden whose only shadow was a wicked serpent. Certainly we know of no people who have lived to nearly 1,000 years, nor in secular history is there any account of a global catastrophe caused by water. Genesis speaks of giants in those days and if the usual interpretation is correct (which I doubt), we must confess also to our ignorance of special humans who are partly the result of the sexual activities of apostate angels. Nor do we know of any towers that so threatened heaven that stark judgment was invoked and executed. No one can deny that Genesis chapters 1–11 are very different to the rest of Genesis, chapters 12–50. The stories of Abraham, Isaac, Jacob, and Joseph are a contrast to the stories of Methuselah, Noah, and the builders of Babel. In the latter section mega incidents impress us by their scarcity.

166

What then? Many of us are fully committed to the fact that Genesis—all of it—is inspired of God and worthy of all acceptance. Again we repeat the solution is simple. How do we explain Luke 16 about the conversation between earth and heaven by the lost and the saved? How do we explain the tormenting flame of the grave scorching the rich man? We know Sodom and Gomorrah are not still burning though once subject to everlasting fire. Adventists have been correct here in not literalizing these stories as many other churches have.

Adventists have tended to be skittish about literature—not without good reason. But there is a penalty sometimes for striving after virtue. The wise man in Ecclesiastes tells us that it is possible (though rare) to be "righteous overmuch" (7:16). Because of our poor acquaintance with literature we tend to be literal-minded and thereby miss a great deal of the depths of Scripture itself. How many Adventists get Christ's point in the parable where those who refuse a wedding invitation are sentenced to death? Or, how many sense the incongruity of the impossible debt mentioned in Matthew 18, or the behaviour of the master in Luke 16:1-8? We even seem able to read such verses as the necessity of eating Christ's flesh and drinking his blood without asking too many questions.

One third of Christ's teachings are parables and metaphors. Usually reference works list 40–50 of these. Obviously a Christ who can speak of men swallowing camels and of the blind leading the blind is not tied to the bonds of literalism. That's why he can liken himself to a door, a vine, a loaf of bread, and the sun (light of the world).

However, we have forgotten that there are parables in the Old Testament also. Many scholars regard the whole book of Jonah as parabolic and Christ's allusion to it is akin to our quotations from Shakespeare. [Equally intelligent scholars do NOT read Jonah as a parable.] Certain it is that most Christians have understood the Song of Songs (*Canticles*) as having more significance than a superficial reading might suggest. But let me ask, what about Genesis chapters 1–11? Are there some similarities between these chapters and Judges 9 and 2 Samuel 12:1-12? We know that some of Christ's stories are aiming at the false religious practises of the Pharisees.

Is Genesis also warning by parables against the prevailing pagan religions of its day?

May I quote again from Foster since by now you are holding it in your hand? He, too, is not infallible, but he is thought provoking:

> There is almost universal scholarly agreement that the Genesis accounts are at least in part polemical documents, designed to contradict the view of the world and the gods enshrined in the competing Mesopotamian and Egyptian religions. It is an anti-polytheistic tract. 'In the beginning, God …' it starts. Not gods and not creatures. The book opens by the clearest possible assertion that there is God (and only one of them), and there are creatures. They are not the same. There is a colossal divide. To worship anything created is to make a basic and terribly dangerous mistake.
>
> The week is redeemed from its bondage to the sky. The Mesopotamians had seven-day lunar cycles, and in obeisance to the moon, the seventh day was a fast day—a day of ill luck. You had it wrong, says the Bible: the seventh day has nothing to do with the moon. And to make the break explicit, the seventh day becomes not a time to fast, fear, and mourn, but a time to celebrate. pages 131–132

Most of the top evangelical scholars today see these controverted chapters as a different literary genre to chapters 12–50 in the same book. For examples see *Old Testament Survey* written by scholars of the Fuller Theological Seminary, or the *Word Biblical Commentary—Genesis 1-15* by Gordon Wenham.

We have already suggested the chief reason that scholars take this stand. Anyone reading Genesis 1–11 senses quite quickly that this is no ordinary literature, and it is not about ordinary events. Probably most of us don't plan on reaching nearly 1,000 years of age. Neither do we expect to build a huge boat about 350 feet long.

One thing that must be taken into account is that Genesis 1–11 reflects many of the current myths of Moses' day. This is particularly true, not only of chapter one, but also of chapters 6 and 7. There are seventeen easily recognizable parallels between the Noah story and existing myths. Scholars are well aware of them. Heidel's classic, *The Gilgamish Epic and Old Testament Parallels* is worthy of our attention. He frankly admits the parallels, but rightly denies that the Genesis story is a mere copy.

This use by Genesis of well-known stories begins with chapter one. Though the chapter is a hundred times saner than those that are next most well known—nevertheless the parallels *are* here. We are forced to ask the question: Was God, in the inspiration of Genesis 1–11, most concerned with history and science, or with the spiritual wellbeing of the first recipients?

Henry Drummond, famous author of *The Greatest Thing in the World* wrote over 100 years ago, but comments written in our own day are remarkably similar. For example, here are some lines from Drummond regarding the first chapters of Genesis:

> There was no science then. Scientific questions were not even asked then. To have given men science would not only have been an anachronism, but a source of mystification and confusion. ... Why was not the use of stars explained to navigators, or chloroform to surgeons? ... What is it to early man to know how the moon was made? What he wants to know is how bread is made. How fish are to be caught, fowls snared, beasts trapped and their skins tanned—these are his problems. ... But that it does not inform us on these practical matters is surely a valid argument why we should not expect it to instruct the world in geology. ... Genesis is a presentation of one or two great elementary truths to the childhood of the world. It can only be read aright in the spirit in which it was written, with its original purpose in view, and its original audience. What did it mean to them? What would they understand by it? What did they need to know and not to know? ... The first principle, which must rule our reading of this book, is the elementary canon of all literary criticism, which decides that any interpretation of a part of a book, or of a literature, must be controlled by the dominant purpose or *motif* of the whole. And when one investigates that dominant purpose in the case of the

Bible, he finds it reducing itself to one thing—religion.
George Adam Smith, *The Life of Henry Drummond*, pages 258-261

Why bother with issues that to many seem esoteric? Because when our children go to university they will soon be disillusioned regarding their childhood inheritance of stories about Noah and the Flood. They will learn that this earth is very, very old as testified by the geologic column as well as radiometric dating and archaeology.

Many of us know families whose children attending university have lost their evangelical faith. The biggest religious Christian group in USA, the Southern Baptists, reported that in over seven years 60 percent of the more than 46,000 churches in the Southern Baptist Convention reported no youth baptisms (ages 12 to 17) in 2012, and eighty percent reported only one or two baptisms among young adults (ages 18-29).

In our own small denomination we too confess that most of our children and youth leave us. That's why this article is important. So many of our churches are filled mainly with old people.

Suppose we could conscientiously teach our families that Genesis 1-11 is as truly inspired as John 1-11, but is a different literary genre— would that not be worth doing? What do we have to lose? On the other hand consider what will most surely be lost if we don't do this?

Our church leaders sigh over our terrible losses but what are we doing about it? Suppose those children you know and love best are carried away by the popular skepticism concerning Genesis, will you feel that the church should have done something to prevent such losses? If so, what?

First, we must approach the inspired text with both care and prayer. It is difficult if not impossible to put away all our preconceived ideas but the danger is lessened when we are aware of our biased state. Then we might ask, 'how have evangelical scholars (who are equally committed to Christ) interpreted these chapters, and what is their evidence?

Consider him who is our example as well as Savior. How much of scientific wisdom did he impart? Indeed, in what areas did he even speak apart from what is needed for our salvation? If he were to speak of science, which science? That of Moses' day, David's day, his own day, our day, or the science to come which alone may be largely accurate?

The main reason many Adventists fear to follow the suggestions here made is that such would seem to diminish the stature of Ellen G. White. Most of our people are unaware that in the last fifty years, SDA scholars have realized that an infallible, inerrant Ellen White is only a myth. Without diminishing her true value we can now confess that her statement "only God and heaven are infallible" fits her also. As far back as the 1970s an article was printed in *Spectrum*, April 1980, written by a top, loyal, Adventist scholar, Donald McAdams. It stated that some facts about E. G. White were now established beyond question: Ellen White used many sources, she was influenced by contemporary writers, and she was not inerrant.

All should read the recent work on Ellen G. White printed by the Oxford University Press and written by both Adventist and non-Adventist scholars.[1] It also is not infallible, but it does give an up-to-date understanding of Ellen G. White as cherished by loyal Adventist researchers.

So what then is our privilege and duty?

Let us teach our children and our church members (many of whom are childlike) that the Bible contains many different types of literature and that all of them are valuable, all are inspired, and all are perfect for their purpose. Not only is there direct prose in the Bible, but poetry, apocalyptic, law, history, parable, and so on. Genesis 1–11, drawing from real events involving real people, has presented the past in parabolic form for religious reasons. Read again Henry Drummond's comments and rejoice to agree with him. In this manner our denomination may be saved from ridicule and rejection and our children from loss of faith.

---

1   Terrie Dopp Aamodt, Gary Land, R. L. Numbers, *Ellen Harmon White: American Prophet,* Oxford, Oxford University Press, 2014.

DARWIN UNDER SCRUTINY

DURING MY YEARS spent at three universities, which required the reading of many scholarly tomes, the most important and unforgettable statement I encountered was the following:

> No matter how original a scholar's imagination, no matter how critical and penetrating his judgment, society does far more of the writing of any book that lives than the author himself.
> C. C. McCown, *The Search for the Real Jesus*, page 18

This pronouncement has enormous bearing on a modern enquiry of tremendous importance. The two most well known books by Charles Darwin—*The Origin of Species* and *The Descent of Man*—have influenced humanity more than any other books of the past thousand years. They are still the center of violent debate. Not only science, but philosophy, religion, politics and ethics are involved. Social Darwinism, war, crime, and the consequences when Christian hope is shattered—these are not trifles but pivots for our age.

Does the society in which Darwin's works were produced cast significant light upon their content and value? Must we believe that nothing produced everything, that chaos produced information, that unconsciousness produced consciousness, that non-life produced life? Or does insight into the genesis of the chief anti-Genesis books demand a pause before the acceptance of the most revolutionary anti-God theory ever invented?

Has Darwinism the right to dominate science and other fields, or has it assumed its primacy by default? Has it conquered because it is the only alternative to Scripture? That is, is it the only game in town? I offer a very simple approach—what were the main factors in Darwin's day and place that influenced his thinking?

Central to Darwinism is the belief that all of nature is one vast battleground teeming with war, struggle, competition, and agony. In the third chapter of his *Origin*, entitled *The Struggle for Existence*, the key word "struggle" occurs over a dozen times in the first four pages. And he tells us in this chapter from whence the idea came. He writes about this concept of universal struggle: "It is the doctrine of Malthus applied with manifold force to the whole animal and vegetable kingdom."

In 1798 Thomas Malthus had written *An Essay on the Principle of Population*. In this he contended that poverty and distress were unavoidable because population increases by geometrical ratio and the means of subsistence by arithmetical ratio. This influenced the economies of governments often resulting in limiting the aid given to the poor and needy. Riots were so spawned, particularly in Darwin's middle years.

However, after decades of influence, Malthus lost his position. Countries are no longer motivated by his philosophy unless engaged in war, famine, or plague. However, Darwin clung to it all his days, and it permeates all that he wrote.

Modern proponents of evolution no longer give primacy to the ideas of competition and struggle. We do find such realities in nature everywhere, but no longer are they considered to be the foremost characteristics of the natural world. Tennyson's words about nature "red in tooth and claw" sprang not from his scientific knowledge but from his grieving over the death of a valued friend.

Most creatures are seed-, plant-, or fruit-eaters and are not carnivores. It is human beings who deliberately and intentionally cause pain as John Burroughs told us long ago. The struggle for existence in the natural world is mainly a bloodless struggle of adaptation. John Burroughs is worth quoting again:

> Nature has an anaesthetic of its own, which she uses in taking life. The carnivorous animals inflict far less pain than appearances would seem to indicate. Tooth and claw usually overwhelm by a sudden blow, and sudden blows benumb and paralyse. Violence in this light is the handmaid of Mercy. If the surgeon

173

could perform his operations in the same sudden and violent manner, an anaesthetic would rarely be needed. ... The soldier in battle may be seriously or fatally wounded and not be aware of it till sometime afterwards.
"The Early Journal Content, *JSTOR*," Vol. 20, *The Auk*

More of Burroughs statement can be found on pages 238-241 of my book larger book, *Genesis Versus Darwinism*. Even Stephen Jay Gould gives an emphasis similar to that of Burroughs in his *Rocks of Ages*, pages 186-187.

Robert E. D. Clark in his *Darwin, Before and After*, page 99 states:

About 99 percent of the cases to which the Darwinian formula has been seriously applied—the individuals, whatever they may be—buds on a tree, young fish in the sea, creeping crawling caterpillars tempting birds to satiate (that hungry feeling)—knew nothing whatever of the struggle in which they were supposed to be engaged.

And G. R. Taylor, well-known and respected evolutionist in his *The Great Evolution Mystery*, page 31 and following: "The assumption of unusual competition is ill founded. ... In fact, competition is rather rare."

Michael Denton tells us that William Paley, long ridiculed, is now coming back into his own. And Paley wrote:

It is a happy world after all. The air, the earth, the water teem with delighted existence. In a spring morn, or a summer evening, on whichever side I turn my eye, myriads of happy beings crowd upon my view.
Natural Theology, page 490

If we turn to a contemporary work such as *The Selfless Gene* by Charles Foster we read:

I was worried that if the only explanation for the complexity, color, and variety of the natural world was the selfishness and struggle intrinsic to the Darwinian natural selection, it was as

immoral to enjoy a walk in the woods as it would be to watch a snuff movie or a piece of extreme sexual sadism.
page xiii

In the same paragraph Foster makes it clear that he is looking particularly at Richard Dawkins, the author of *The Selfish Gene*. And in rebutting that book Foster points out that nature is ruled more by altruism than by bitter bloody struggle. Again we quote him:

Sociability, cooperation, and apparent altruism are commonplace in nature. Birds flock, ungulates herd, insects build cooperative communities of immense sociological complexity, fish swim in shoals, and humans build cities, trade, and go to football games.
page 97.

He proceeds by offering the example of the mole rat and adds an appropriate comment from Darwin's classic:

The naked mole rat of East Africa lives in large underground colonies. One of them, the queen, grows to a colossal size and is served by the others, who are celibate workers. The workers' devotion to the colony seems, depending on your point of view, tear-jerkingly admirable or plain pathological. Sometimes they will die for the colony, blocking a tunnel with their own body to stop a snake getting in.

The naked mole rat was the sort of animal that kept Darwin awake at night:

Natural selection cannot possibly produce any modification in any one species exclusively for the good of another species, though throughout nature, one species incessantly takes advantage of, and profits by, the structure of another. ... If it could be proved that any part of the structure of any one species had been formed for the exclusive good of another species, it would annihilate my theory, for such could not have been produced through natural selection.
The Origin of Species, chapter 6

Foster thinks Darwin may have been too hard on himself and his theory. I wonder. Readers using the Internet can find other writers on this topic of altruism, which challenges the views of Richard Dawkins and others.

Not only have Darwin's central ideas of struggle and competition come to their end with none to help them, but his other main pillars for organic evolution also have been felled. Pangenesis—his strange insupportable theory on heredity—lasted for some few years until the ideas of Gregor Mendel were universally understood in the 1930's. With the demise of pangenesis came challenges to gradualism, absolute uniformitarianism, survival of the fittest, and sexual selection. (See my expanded book for the evidence.) Since then mathematicians have questioned the more recent views regarding mutations.

These facts validate Darwin's confession to Thomas Huxley that his book was "a mere rag of a hypothesis with as many flaws and holes as sound parts." (See Janet Browne's *Charles Darwin, the Power of Place*, page 53.)

There is another area that should at least be touched upon—the multiple factors of British culture that impinged on Darwin. The age was one with emphasis on progress, machinery, colonialism, industrialization, and increasing education. This explains why Harvard historian Browne states: "Darwinism was made by Darwin and Victorian society." See page xi of the first of her two volumes of Darwin's biography.

The theory of evolution was not novel with Darwin. Long before the publication of *The Origin* evolution was talked about in the streets of London and elsewhere. His grandfather had written *Zoonomia*, a medico-evolutionary book, and in 1844 Robert Chambers had published *Vestiges*, an evolutionary view of the universe, and even these were not the originators of the theory. There is, indeed, nothing new under the sun.

Even Darwin's racial attitudes reflected those of his society. He believed the burgeoning of the white races would eradicate the black. He also held tenaciously to the nineteenth-century view of the role of the sexes. Woman was intended for childbearing, not for scholastic reflection. For further evidence see *Darwin* by Adrian Desmond and James Moore, particularly pages 579 to 581. The writer's comment on *The Descent of Man* is as follows:

> In many ways the book was the man-pudgy and comfortable, sedate in its seniority, full of anecdote and rather old-fashioned. There was little fire and flair about it .... It did not tax one's tolerance so much as entertain. It told an arm-chair adventure of the English evolving, clambering up from the apes, struggling to conquer savagery, multiplying and dispersing around the globe ... habituated on material progress, social mobility, and imperial adventure.

I venture to hope that the reader will buy Desmond and Moore's *Descent of Man* and read the quintessence of their case. This book is the best recent publication about Darwin. The authors demonstrate that the old way of telling Darwin's story has gone forever. No longer is he viewed as a superb genius towering above his fellows. Instead, he is rightly presented as an excellent example of his time and place with all the inevitable minuses that involves.

The most important question for today is: Has the theory of organic evolution achieved its widespread acceptance because of its overwhelming evidence, or because "it is the only game in town" if Scripture is despised?

Intelligent Christians concur with much that is found in *The Origin of Species*—all that has to do with microevolution (changes within species, such as the multiplicity of canine kinds). However, innumerable scientists who are not Christians find Darwin's case for macroevolution (changes involving *phyla*) still only hypothetical. Therefore, there will always be many who believe that the pervading ill consequences of faith in Darwin had their origin not in certified truth but, at least in some cases, in uncertified guesses.

Answer me—Where Are the Myriads of Living Intermediate Forms?

THIS ARTICLE IS an attempt to anticipate and refute certain criticisms of the larger version of my book, *Genesis Versus Darwinism (GVD)*. My chief protest is that most critics and critiques pass by the evidence of those chapters in the heart of *GVD* that discuss paleontology and the fossil record. See chapters 12, 13, 19-22, 23, and 24.

The chief objection on the grounds of science made against *The Origin of Species* on its appearance was that the transitional forms demanded by the theory were nowhere to be found. Darwin anticipates the objection and refers to it in several places, especially in chapters six and nine. His main defence is "the imperfection of the geological record," which is the title of his ninth chapter.

But today that defence has evaporated and is rarely invoked, and when the subject is addressed, it is only by the ignorant or dishonest. Ridley, an Oxford biologist states, "no real evolutionist, whether gradualist or punctuationist, uses the fossil record as evidence in favour of the theory of evolution" ("Who Doubts Evolution?" *New Scientist*, Vols. 830, 831, 1981, page 90). This is in spite of the fact that it has always been customary to say, as Theodosius Dobzhansky—a noted geneticist and evolutionary biologist—has told us, that the main case for evolution is in the fossil record.

Is this issue central or peripheral? Considering that even Darwin admitted that his theory demanded "infinitely numerous," "innumerable," "countless," "inconceivably great" numbers of transitional intermediate forms, it is obvious that the issue is indeed central. All arguing for Darwinism must deal with this question.

Darwin's argument regarding the imperfection of the fossil record may have impressed some in his day, but it impresses no geologist and no paleoanthropologist today. No one now denies that over

200 million fossil specimens have been catalogued. These cover over 250,000 fossil species. It is almost universally admitted now that both Darwin and Charles Lyell (a contemporary of Darwin and the foremost geologist of his day) were wrong in their insistence on geological imperfections. It is just not true that the fossil record is woefully incomplete. For practical purposes it *is* complete as the testimonies of geologists prove.

Michael Denton writes:

> Considering that the total number of known fossil species is nearly one hundred thousand, the fact that the only relatively convincing morphological sequences are *a handful of cases like the horse*, which do not involve a great deal of change, and which in many cases like the elephant may not even present phylogenetic sequences at all, serves to emphasize the *remarkable lack of any direct evidence* for major evolutionary transformations in the fossil record.
> *Evolution: a Theory in Crisis*, p. 185 *(emphasis ours)*

The quest to discover phylogenies has failed:

> Darwinian theory asserts that physical descent with modification has been universal, which means that every modern species is the latest link in a phylogeny. There must therefore have been hundreds of thousands of phylogonies, and it was Darwin's belief that these would be found. His followers, sharing his expectation, felt a duty to seek and find the phylogenies. ...
>
> The expectations were vain. The zeal came to naught. In the 125 years since the *Origin* nothing has been accomplished. *No phylogenies have been established* and the pursuit of them has fallen into disrepute. The following authorities attest to this.
> E. Saiff and N. Macbeth, "Evolution" (unpublished manuscript, 1982), cited by Bird, *The Origin of Species Revisited*, Vol. 1., page 188

Mayr, acknowledged dean of evolutionists writes:

> The futile attempts to establish the relationship of the major

phyla of animals induced at least one competent zoologist at the turn of the century to deny common descent. Fleischmann (1901) called the theory a beautiful myth not substantiated by any factual foundation. Kerkut, fifty years later, does not draw such an extreme conclusion but he is almost equally pessimistic about ever achieving an understanding of the relationship of the higher animal taxa. Honesty compels us to admit that *our ignorance concerning these relationships is still great, not to say overwhelming.* This is a depressing state of affairs. ...
The Growth of Biological Thought, 1982, page 218 *(emphasis ours)*

A well-known letter from Dr. Colin Patterson replying to one of his critics is very significant:

I fully agree with your comments on the lack of illustration of evolutionary transitions in my book. If I knew of any, fossil or living, I would certainly have included them. ... I will lay it on the line—there is not one such fossil for which one could make a watertight argument. The reason is that statements about ancestry and descent are not applicable in the fossil record.
Letter to Luther D. Sunderland, April 10, 1979, cited in *The Origin of Species Revisited,* Vol. 1, page 59

David Woodruff speaks similarly: "the record fails to contain a single example of a significant transition" *(Evolution: The Paleobiological View,* Vol. 208, *Science,* 1980, page 716).

Gould, of course, had given the whole game away earlier when he wrote: "The extreme rarity of transitional forms in the fossil record persists as the trade secret of paleontology" ("Evolution's Erratic Pace," *Natural History,* May 1977, pages 12,14).

I have repeatedly challenged Darwinians to read Denton's chapter "The Fossil Record" in his book *Evolution: A Theory in Crisis.* Here is a quotation from that book:

Even if a number of species were known to biology which were indeed perfectly intermediate, possessing organ systems that were unarguably transitional in the sense required by evolution,

this would certainly not be sufficient to validate the evolutionary model of nature. To refute typology and securely validate evolutionary claims would necessitate hundreds or even thousands of different species, all unambiguously intermediate in terms of their overall biology and the physiology and anatomy of all their organ systems.
page 117

The idea that fossils provide evidence for Darwinism is a myth, as Patterson, Raup, and many others have forthrightly declared. And it is because of this undeniable fact that I venture to criticize my critics who speak of many things but rarely of this conundrum.

There is another main area that I have touched upon in the larger *GVD* (see pages 276, 306, and 369) that is also neglected by modern Darwinian protagonists. The whole world of nature has been transformed in the thinking of research scientists since the middle of last century. The discoveries of microbiology have devastated any claims that chance could have originated life and its subsequent forms. We now know that even algae and fungi have unbelievable amounts of information behind their arrival. It is even somewhat humiliating to learn that a salamander has more information necessary for its birth than a human being.

Fred Hoyle and Chandra Wickramasinghe have emphasized this in their small volume *Evolution from Space*. I quote at some length certain of their primary reminders:

With the development of microbiology in the second half of the twentieth century it became overwhelmingly clear that the truth is quite otherwise [compared to earlier scientific views]. Biochemical systems are exceedingly complex, so much so that the chance of their being formed through random shufflings of simple organic molecules is exceedingly minute, to a point where it is insensibly different from zero.
page xv

Ancient life-forms discovered in the rocks do not reveal a simple beginning. Although we may care to think of fossil bacteria and

fossil algae and microfungi as being simple compared to a dog or a horse, the information standard remains enormously high.
page xxi

[How was it that the] highly specific enzymes needed for the repair process came to be present in the bacteria …?
page 17

The enzymes are a large class of molecule that for the most part runs across the whole of biology, without there being any hint of their mode of origin.
page 19

The trouble is that there are about two thousand enzymes, and the chance of obtaining them all in a random trial is only one part in $(10^{20})^{2,000} = 10^{40,000}$, an outrageously small probability that could not be faced even if the whole universe consisted of organic soup.
page 20

The revulsion which biologists feel to the thought that purpose might have a place in the structure of biology is therefore revulsion to the concept that biology might have a connection to an intelligence higher than our own.
page 30

It is ironic that the scientific facts throw Darwin out, but leave William Paley, a figure of fun to the scientific world for more than a century, still in the tournament with a chance of being the ultimate winner.
page 102

Our point of view is anti-Darwinian and is in a sense a return to the concept of special creation. … We have received hints and even warnings from friends and colleagues that our views on these matters are generally repugnant to the scientific world. We in our turn have been disturbed to discover how little attention is generally paid to fact and how much to myths and prejudice.
page 163

(Hoyle was not an evangelical Christian and believed in panspermia).

> Darwinian evolution is most unlikely to get even one polypeptide right, let alone the thousands on which living cells depend for their survival. This situation is well-known to geneticists and yet nobody seems prepared to blow the whistle decisively on the theory. ... life cannot have had a random beginning ... prior information was necessary to produce a living cell.
> pages 164-165

> We have emphasized the enormous information content of even the simplest living systems. The information cannot in our view be generated by what are often called 'natural' processes. ... We have argued that the requisite information came from an 'intelligence.'
> page 166

> The general scientific world has been bamboozled into believing that evolution has been proved. Nothing could be further from the truth.
> page 92

On page 85 the writers are equally scathing as they repudiate Darwin's contention that the fossil record was incomplete.

This evidence from highly credentialed scientists is in accord with the scientific argument of *Genesis versus Darwinism (GVD)*. It is perfectly proper and even a duty that many should question the conclusions of *GVD*, but it is not proper to ignore certain of it emphases. Both the religious and the scientific world suffer from the fear of being "out of step" with the majority. Such people need the reminder that the greatest contributions to human wellbeing have come from nonconformists.

[I heartily recommend the recent book *The Information Paradox* by Robert Wiles.]

"Adventists don't eat pork and hate Catholics!"

MANY OF US have heard the crude summary often made about Adventists. "They're the people who don't eat pork and hate Catholics." Dale Carnegie would have been horrified. Apparently, here is a Christian group that has not done a very good job of winning friends and influencing people. As Adventists, we have a very poor reputation with the largest of all Christian bodies—Roman Catholicism—as well as with many Protestant groups also. We have earned that stigma because for over a century and a half we have inaccurately labelled the present papacy as the Antichrist of Scripture.

Consider the most formidable of all our publications that has bearing on this topic—L. E. Froom's *The Prophetic Faith of our Fathers*. I remember once at Manchester University Professor F. F. Bruce warning me not to be too elaborate on a certain topic in case I duplicated Froom's example. Dr. Froom's whole intent was to justify Historicism with its anti-papal emphasis.

But what are the facts on this matter? Is the Papacy the Antichrist of Scripture? Were the Reformers right or wrong in their opinion on this matter? Has exegesis of Scripture yielded more insights in recent decades than in previous centuries?

There are some obvious facts that should be kept in mind. Antichrist is only mentioned by that name in the Epistles of John. He declares that in his day there were many antichrists (1 John 2:18). But John also wrote that Antichrist was yet to come. See 1 John 2:18 and 4:3. Therefore, we have Scripture for the fact that the title has more than a single application. [Ellen White also taught that all who oppose Christ have earned this label. See the *Seventh-day Adventist Bible Commentary (SDABC)*, Volume 7, page 950, first edition: "Antichrist, meaning all who exalt themselves against the will and work of God."]

This should not surprise us. The very first prophecy of Scripture, Genesis 3:15, is applied in the New Testament to more than one event. See Romans 16:20 and Revelation 12:17. Similarly, most readers of Matthew 24 have concluded that it applied both to the end of Jerusalem and its temple and to the end of the world. The *SDABC* in commenting on the "apostasy," linked with the "man of sin" in 2 Thessalonians 2, states that it "was partially fulfilled in Paul's day, and much more so during the Dark Ages, but its complete fulfilment occurs in the days immediately prior to the return of Jesus" (Volume 7, page 270, 1st edn).

Another well known instance of recurring fulfilment is found in Joel 2:28, which according to its context belongs to the very last days, yet Peter applied it to the day of Pentecost in the first century. See Acts 2:16-18. There are many other examples in Scripture of recurring fulfilments including Isaiah 7:14 (according to the *SDABC*). Some say that this principle does not apply to the apocalyptic books like Daniel and Revelation but few exegetes see any light in that claim. It is obvious that Daniel 9:24-27 was conditional. Had the Jews accepted their Messiah, Jerusalem would never have been destroyed.

Seventh-day Adventists throughout most of their history have dogmatically claimed that the little horn of Daniel 8 could not possibly be Antiochus Epiphanes. George McCready Price, however, saw in Antiochus what he called an apotelesmatic fulfilment. See his *The Greatest of the Prophets*, pages 30-31. At the 1919 Bible Conference there was a lengthy, apparently positive discussion about Antiochus Epiphanes, beginning with a comment by William G. Wirth, a teacher at Pacific Union College in Angwin, California: "It seems to me that Antiochus Epiphanes is really the great figure in this chapter." [1]

In 1977 the fate of my commentary on Daniel was being decided in Washington DC. Dr. Siegfried Horn with more than characteristic vigour stated that to fail to see Antiochus as a first fulfilment of the little horn of Daniel 8 was a ridiculous mistake and contrary to the

---

[1]   This can be read at: 'Report of Bible Conference for July 7, 1919,' pages 65-66, and July 8, 1919, pages 18-27, published in the SDA Church online document archive. http://www.adventistarchives.org/search … =antiochus.

exegetes of all centuries. The Adventist failure in this regard was motivated by its doctrine of Antichrist. We were intent on finding the papacy in Daniel 8, come what may!

Christ's prophecy of Matthew 24 draws from Daniel chapters 7, 8, 9, 11, and 12. Exegetes for twenty centuries have affirmed that Christ saw in the looming events of A.D. 70 a larger fulfilment of the crisis first initiated by Antiochus Epiphanes in 167 B.C., when he defiled the temple by sacrificing a pig upon its altar (anathema to the Jews).

But in recent times scholars have insisted that the Greek use of a masculine participle linked with a neuter noun in Mark 13:14 [referring to the words "standing" and "abomination"] indicates a yet larger fulfilment than the initial one of the Roman armies devastating the Jewish temple. Usually such scholars link Mark 13:14 with 2 Thessalonians 2 and its warning about "the man of sin."

In the eschatological crises depicted in Revelation, all the classical commentaries on Revelation see allusions to Daniel's portrayal of the little horn and the wilful king (Daniel chapters 7, 8, 9, 11, and 12), and most of them state that the events of the days of Antiochus Epiphanes were only a type of later more comprehensive fulfilments of Daniel's "little horn."

I spent 1971 and 1972 at Manchester University studying all that was considered of value in classical commentaries on Daniel, Matthew, 2 Thessalonians and Revelation, as well as the relevant Scriptures.[2] The University Press of America published my thesis, and it is now recommended in sundry reference works such as the *New Dictionary of Theology*. My conclusions have much in common with those later published by Dr. Reinder Bruinsma, although his emphasis was historical rather than exegetical.

In summary, the Antichrist chapters have their "seed" in Daniel, their "blade" in the Olivet sermon, their "ear" in 2 Thessalonians, and

---

2   My Manchester thesis, "The Abomination of Desolation in Biblical Eschatology," written under the supervision of Professor F. F. Bruce, is housed in many Seminary libraries and contains hundreds of references to available books on the topics of this article. These substantiate the positions here taken.

their "full corn in the ear" in Revelation. All these are consistent in warning against wicked powers inspired and empowered by Satan against Christ, his gospel, and his people.

The climactic chapters on the antichrist theme are Revelation 12 and 13. Here we have a counterfeit Trinity—Satan (counterfeit of God the Father), the sea beast (a false Messiah) and the two-horned lamblike creature (a false prophet). In Revelation 12:9-13 we are referred back to Calvary where the decisive struggle between Satan (the chief Antichrist) and Christ took place. Colossians 2:15 reveals that on Calvary Christ overthrew principalities and powers. This was the first and chief Armageddon including heavenly signs, earthquake, and resurrections. Now Antichrist and his brood are defeated foes despite their continued activity.

The second figure in Revelation 13, the two-horned lamblike beast, the false prophet, has nothing to do with the United States, despite J. N. Andrews and his successors' affirmations. Throughout the Old Testament we constantly have the anti-god leaders in couples—Balak and Balaam, Ahab and Jezebel, Absalom and Ahithtophel, and here in Revelation 13 that trend is continued. Usually the leading member of the couplet is a secular ruler, and the second a religious but apostate figure. The first readers of Revelation identified the two companions of Satan as the Roman Government and the religious leaders of the time who supported that government.

The vast majority of commentators for 2,000 years have emphasized that interpretation. But like many of the apocalyptic prophecies the meaning in following centuries has remained the same in principle but different in identification. Thus the Reformers saw the union of church and state in the medieval centuries as antichrist, and they were correct. The final fulfilment is yet to be, but again it will take place when the sea beast (human government) and the two-horned lamblike figure (apostate religion) join together under Satanic control. There is no other legitimate way of interpreting Revelation 13.

Why does it matter to attempt to interpret these Scriptural figures? First, it matters because a right conclusion should tell us the truth about the world in which we live and guide us in our decision-making. Second, false interpretations not only shear us of spiritual strength (like Samson's loss of his strength-giving hair), but they can falsify the gospel in spirit and in truth. Error can invite unnecessary antagonism from those with whom we covet amity.

May I call again upon Him who is Lord of Lords and King of Kings? Jesus, in his great prophetic sermon (almost the size of the Sermon on the Mount) used the well-known danielic phrase "the abomination of desolation" for antichrist. See Matthew 24:15. The first term "abomination," always concerns apostate religion. See its frequent Old Testament usage. The second term, both in its context and in its original language, signifies threatening force from worldly powers. The term "abomination of desolation" first appeared in connection with Daniel's "little horn" of chapters 7 and 8.

Antiochus Epiphanes was not only a brutal king, but also a mad religionist. Keep in mind that the idea of the little horns of chapters 7 and 8 being different cannot be sustained. Jewish scholars in the years before Christ interpreted the fourth beast of Daniel 7 as Syria and Antiochus as its king. The Apocrypha agrees. Only in later years did Christians read Rome rather than Syria (see 2 Esdras 12:11-13).

It should be of special interest to Adventists that Daniel 8:14, 9:24 and 7:13,14 are linked by exegetes as pointing to the same reality—the end of time, the destruction of all evil, and the triumph of God over all evil. Each of these passages assure us that the triumph of the abominable little horn is only temporary and that the coming of the kingdom of glory will eradicate it, vindicate God and cleanse the universe from all sin. (See my *The Abomination of Desolation in Biblical Eschatology*, page 136.)

It has too often been missed, but the historical chapters of Daniel are the key to its prophetic passages. Nebuchadnezzar, Belshazzar, and Darius act out historically what coming antichrists would do on a much larger scale. Their features in common are blasphemy, idolatry, and persecution. Always government and bad religion unite in order to eviscerate opposition. We have no right to apply the term antichrist to any religious power that does not use civil government in order to persecute those who disagree with it.

188

The final Antichrist (the "trinity" in Revelation chapters 12 and 13) will proscribe the flock of Christ in the last days and execute many, but the promise of Scripture is that the returning Christ will deliver those of his threatened people who have survived the last conflict. Note the use of the word "deliver" in Daniel 12:1 and compare with it Daniel 3:17 and 6:20,27. So Revelation 14:1-5 pictures a victorious company surviving the threatened holocaust of Revelation 13.

Adventists have done well to be vitally interested in the prophecies of Daniel and Revelation, but we settled too early on questionable interpretations. The mistake has been costly, and until we correct it our name will be "mud" with many who truly adore Christ.

The rest of the Protestant world (I generalize) has given up its anti-Catholic thrust. Should not we? If in surveying the globe we fail to see the papacy universally united with governments in order to execute nonconformists (as in the Middle Ages), we have no biblical ground for labelling it as a manifestation of antichrist. There are millions of Christian saints in the Catholic Church who love Christ supremely and will certainly be in his kingdom. The deserved ill impression we give others is unnecessary and not Christian.

We denounce the moral lapses of many priests, the church's acceptance of Darwinism, and its errors regarding important biblical doctrines—such as its views on baptism, the Lord's Supper, the nature of man and the state of the dead, Sunday as the Sabbath, their wrong view of righteousness by faith, Mariolatry, etc. However, these do not make Catholicism the antichrist of Scripture any more than Adventism's manifold errors of prophetic exposition such as the Investigative Judgment and its misuse of Ellen G. White make it an emissary of Satan.

Luther was very wise when he said "Pope self is what I fear most." May God help us to emulate him in this important matter and wipe our slate clean of traditional but inaccurate and uncharitable prophetic expositions.

SIX-THOUSAND-YEAR CREATIONISM—
WHAT SHALL WE DO WITH ELLEN G. WHITE AND GEORGE MCCREADY PRICE?

ELLEN WHITE USES the prevailing chronological figure of 6,000 years or nearly 6,000 years many times when speaking of the reign of sin. In one place she states, "for over 6,000 years" (*Christian Temperance and Bible Hygiene,* page 154), and in another place she writes, "more than six thousand years" (*Signs of the Times,* 29 Sep. 1887). However, what else could she have said at the time?

Bill Bryson tells us, "Human beings would split the atom and invent television, nylon, and instant coffee before they could figure out the age of their own planet" (*A Short History of Nearly Everything,* page 55).

It is also true that by the middle of the nineteenth century well-educated people considered the planet to be at least a few million years old. But they were not the primary audience for which Ellen White was writing. And Ellen White was hardly well educated.

Charles Darwin desperately needed to have an old earth, but he lacked the means of proving the ages he desired. However, "such was the confusion that by the close of the nineteenth century, depending on which text you considered, you could learn that the number of years that stood between us and the dawn of complex life in the Cambrian period was 3 million, 18 million, 600 million, 794 million, or 2.4 billion." (*Ibid.*, pages 84-85).

It was only in 1953 that Dr. Clair Cameron Patterson, twentieth-century geologist, came up with the number of 4,550 million years, a number that stands virtually unchallenged now in the twenty-first century.

Of course, most Christians had their Authorized Version of the

Bible, which often included the calculations of Archbishop James Ussher, based erroneously on the assumption that the biblical genealogies were complete and intended as gauges for ascertaining how long man had lived on earth. Today nobody in the field of biblical chronology holds to the errors of Ussher, even though he was a brilliant scholar for his time. However, Ellen White wrote most of her books more than a century and a half before the careful scientific work of Clair Patterson. She really only had Ussher to follow.

George McCready Price (1870-1963) was a devotee of Ellen White and viewed her writings to be almost as infallible as the Bible itself. Because he lived for some decades after the death of White, and because he was a voracious reader, he ultimately came to believe in a very old earth. But in his earlier books we find no such conviction.

The comparatively recent fundamentalist contentions for a young earth sprang originally from Ellen White, via McCready Price. Whitcomb and Morris's *The Genesis Flood* (1961) remained for over fifty years the scientific Bible for fundamentalists, including Seventh-day Adventists. However, the burgeoning of work in geology and paleontology has made the views of Whitcomb and Morris completely untenable.

Men may dispute certain arguments used for an old earth, but their endeavours are like those of blind men who, in touching a tree here and there, contend that there was no forest. Today there are over fifty well-established methods for proving an old earth. Anyone who studies the Geologic Column with its successive strata over billions of years is left without doubt regarding the earth's age.

The matter of the origin of complex life forms is a more difficult matter and usually is located about half a billion years ago. The successive strata of the Geologic Column begin with minute life forms such as snails, algae and bacteria. But as one moves up the Column, life forms become more and more complicated, and we never find the less complex groups prevailing. We do not find a rabbit among the algae before the Cambrian rocks, and we do not find human skeletons halfway up the Column.

191

Why did our Lord and Saviour not inform men regarding the scientific facts, which are now almost universally accepted? The answer is because he was engaged in something much more important. Like Moses and the prophets before him, his interest lay in the right relationship between God and man. We should not look in any book for that which God has not promised to provide.

As we make decisions it is very difficult to avoid the extremes. It is just not true to say, "wrong in one, therefore wrong in all". Everything human is mixed. Price's *The Greatest of the Prophets* is much superior to anything Uriah Smith ever wrote. However, like all his readers, Price was fallible. Books like *Steps to Christ* and *The Desire of Ages* surpass anything else in Adventist literature. The *Conflict of the Ages* series has many of the scattered gems of truth White said should be gathered up. Thank God for these books, but don't use them as Bibles, because that they are not.

I was expelled from ministry because I disagreed with Ellen G. White on the Investigative Judgment. I was aware she had copied from Uriah Smith and others on that topic though she improved them all. I still disagree with her conclusions on this topic. But I have to remember that to live a lie for over 70 years is far beyond most of us. Then, I have to recall Ellen White's other ministry— preaching. Horace John Shaw, whom I knew and valued, wrote what is perhaps the best book on that topic, his dissertation on rhetoric for Michigan State University, entitled "A Historical Analysis of the Speaking of Mrs Ellen G. White, a Pioneer and Spokeswoman of the Seventh-day Adventist Church."

Ellen White often preached to thousands, and H. M. S. Richards has testified to the electrical impact her presentations often made. Even after 1909 she still travelled and spoke frequently. In her early 80's she crossed the continent giving scores of addresses. In 1909 she made a five-month journey to the Eastern States speaking 72 times in 27 different places. Those of you who often engage in public speaking are well aware of its personal cost and demand, and the number of effectual speakers diminishes with the march of years. Furthermore, while Ellen White's accusers suggest she could not write well (I do not agree with this), we are confronted with the evidence that she had no difficulty in marshalling words for huge audiences.

I have spent many hours in the stacks of the Library of Congress. Every kind of writing before the twentieth century found there uses a variety of sources without credit. It was only in 1909 that Congress enacted the first comprehensive copyright law. Those who condemn Ellen White for plagiarism often use such works as Matthew Henry's *Bible Commentary* or the sermons of Charles H. Spurgeon. Both these authors borrowed very heavily from preceding authors.

There is an important factor that cannot and should not be ignored. At the time of the Minneapolis Conference in 1888 Ellen White seemed to undergo a second conversion. Thereafter, whenever she wrote on the gospel and the Christian life, her teaching was an excellent reproduction of the righteousness of faith taught in the Pauline Epistles. Here are some examples from *Selected Messages*, Volume 1, pages 350-400:

> We must learn in the school of Christ. Nothing but his righteousness can entitle us to any one of the blessings of the covenant of grace. We have long desired and tried to obtain these blessings, but have not received them because we have cherished the idea that we could do something to make ourselves worthy of them. We have not looked away from ourselves, believing that Jesus is a living Saviour. ... We must believe the naked promise, and not accept feeling for faith. When we trust God fully, when we rely upon the merit of Jesus as a sin-pardoning Saviour, we shall receive all the help that we can desire.

> We look to self, as though we had power to save ourselves; but Jesus died for us because we are helpless to do this. In him is our hope, our justification, our righteousness. ...

> My brethren, are you expecting that your merit will recommend you to the favour of God, thinking that you must be free from sin before you trust his power to save? If this is the struggle going on in your mind, I fear you will gain no strength, and will finally become discouraged.
> page 351

Come to Jesus, and receive rest and peace. You may have the blessing even now. ... He is my righteousness, and my crown of rejoicing.
page 352

We can do nothing, absolutely nothing, to commend ourselves to divine favour. We must not trust at all to ourselves, nor to our good works, but when as erring, sinful beings we come to Christ, we may find rest in his love. God will accept every one that comes to him trusting wholly in the merits of a crucified Saviour.
pages 353-354. ...

The fact that Christ is our righteousness, which seemed to souls who were hungry for truth, as light too precious to be received.
page 356

The tidings that Christ is our righteousness has brought relief to many, many souls. ...
page 357

The thought that the righteousness of Christ is imputed to us not because of any merit on our part, but as a free gift from God seemed a precious thought.
page 360

The law demands righteousness, and this the sinner owes to the law, but he is incapable of rendering it. The only way in which he can attain to righteousness is through faith. By faith he can bring to God the merits of Christ, and the Lord places the obedience of his Son to the sinner's account. Christ's righteousness is accepted in place of man's failure, and God receives, pardons, justifies the repentant, believing soul, treats him as though he were righteous, and loves him as he loves his own Son. This is how faith is accounted righteousness.
page 367

In looking to Christ, we shall see that his love is without a parallel, that he has taken the place of the guilty sinner, and has imputed unto him his spotless righteousness.
page 374

When it is in the heart to obey God, when efforts are put forth to this end, Jesus accepts this disposition and efforts as man's best service, and he makes up for the deficiency with his own divine merit.
page 382

When God pardons the sinner, remits the punishment he deserves, and treats him as though he had not sinned, he receives him into divine favour, and justifies him through the merits of Christ's righteousness. ... Faith is the only condition upon which justification can be obtained, and faith includes not only belief, but trust.
page 389

It is God that circumcises the heart. The whole work is the Lord's from beginning to the end. The perishing sinner may say: ... I need not remain a single moment longer unsaved." ...

The great work that is wrought for the sinner who is spotted and stained by evil is the work of justification. By him who speaketh truth he is declared righteous. The Lord imputes unto the believer the righteousness of Christ and pronounces him righteous before the universe.
page 392

Christ is the end of the law for righteousness to everyone who believeth. In ourselves we are sinners, but in Christ we are righteous.
page 394

They are not to look forward thinking that at some future time a great work is to be done for them, for the work is now complete. The believer is not called upon to make his peace with God; he never has nor ever can do this. He is to accept Christ as his peace, for with Christ is God and peace.
page 395

No man of himself can repent, and make himself worthy of the blessing of justification. ... We cannot take a step toward spiritual life save as Jesus draws and strengthens the soul, and leads us to experience that repentance that need not be repented of. ... Repentance is no less the gift of God than are pardon and justification, and it cannot be experienced except as it is given to the soul by Christ. pages 390-391

It is my conviction that no one could write these lines unless the reality spoken of had been personally experienced.

As for George McCready Price, again extremes should be shunned. Anyone who has read Price is convicted the author was intelligent and a very able writer. However, he was not a trained geologist and had practically no field experience. His views sprang from Ellen White who had inherited them from other Christians of her century. His books on evolution are not entirely without merit but read today are very inadequate. Unless one is correct regarding the Geologic Column it is impossible to make a consistent case against Darwinism.

It is not true that Price was so dogmatic as to never change his mind. His original views of a young earth did change. People who knew Price intimately for the most part respected him and liked him. His students found him sympathetic and Christian in his daily behaviour. His reputation for spotless moral integrity has never been successfully challenged. He often worked 18-hour days and he wrote not for gold, but for what he thought was the glory of God. I began reading his books in 1944 and corresponded with him in the 1950s.

Of no person can it be said what Paul wrote concerning Scripture—that it is given by inspiration of God and is reliable for doctrine, for reproof, for correction, for instruction in righteousness that the man of God may be perfect, thoroughly furnished unto all good works (2 Tim. 3:16,17).

We can thank God for tireless Christian workers like White and Price, and there are things we can learn from them, but the idolatry of infallibility should never be laid at their door. The suggestion of a 6,000-year age of the earth was a misinterpretation in 1650, and time has not vindicated Ussher's calculations 465 years later.

Exodus 20: 8-11—The Literal Application of "God Made the Heavens and the Earth in Six Days"

EXODUS 20: 8-11 is clear and emphatic that God made the world in six days. And God is the speaker. Why should any doubt the literal meaning of these verses? This is an excellent and important enquiry. Consider these comments:

> At best, all language about God is analogical. Words used to describe him and his acts must inevitably be human words, but they do not have quite the same meaning when applied to him as when they refer to men. In speaking of God as father, we do not assign him all the attributes of human fatherhood. Similarly, in speaking of him creating the world in six days, we do not identify his mode of creation with human creativity nor need we assume his week's work was necessarily accomplished in 144 hours. By speaking of six days of work followed by one day's rest, Genesis 1 draws attention to the correspondence between God's work and man's and God's rest as a model for the Sabbath, but that does not necessarily imply that the six days of creation are the same as human days.
> Gordon J. Wenham, *Word Biblical Commentary*, Genesis 1-15, page 40

The truthfulness of the above is not hard to recognize when we consider the many statements regarding God that are purely anthropomorphic. God is spoken of in Scripture as "repenting," as "breathing," as the Maker of a crafty wicked serpent, as making clothing, and so on. But the New Testament is clear when it tells us that God is spirit and one who is changeless (John 4:24; Heb. 13:8). But see such passages as Genesis 6:7; 1 Samuel 15:11; and Jonah 4:2. Translators have seen the difficulty and often take out "repent," instead using a softer term. In Cruden's *Concordance* we read:

> When the word [repent] is used of God it is a figure of speech, which speaks of him almost as if human; and since his actions

are changed, attributes to him the feelings which, in a man, would cause such a change.

A key to Exodus 20:8-11 is its reference to God's rest. Put with this Exodus 31:17 which says that "in six days the Lord made heaven and earth, and on the seventh day he rested, and was refreshed."

Scripture also tells us that the omnipotent God is never weary (Isa. 40:28) and therefore to speak of him as being "refreshed" is purely anthropomorphic. We cannot take the word "rested" in Exodus 20:11 literally, or we contradict the Bible. Similarly, with the rest of the verse. God is talking to his ignorant children in terms that could be understood at that early age of civilization.

Jewish Rabbis believed that the chief purpose of Genesis 1 was to give importance to the Sabbath, and many Christian commentators have agreed. Once we recognize that Genesis 1 with its message of the universe being made in less than a week with the heavenly orbs only being created after this planet, we have no difficulty with Exodus 20:8-11. See also Genesis 2:1. In neither reference (Genesis nor Exodus) is God trying to teach his people precise science.

John 5:17 denies that God ever rests. He is always at work for the sake of his children. When we recognize that God is ever condescending to talk to us in our terms and for practical purposes the inevitable presence of anthropomorphisms will not trouble us. The Decalogue, like Genesis 1 was given for practical purposes, not for purposes of teaching either science or history.

CHRIST AND CALVARY:
PAST, PRESENT, FUTURE—
BEGINNING, CENTER, END

*Jesus is ever central, between the Father and the Spirit,
between time and eternity, between law and grace,
between us and condemnation and death.*

NO ONE HAS ever plumbed the heights and depths of that day that redeemed us from eternal loss and procured for believers their eternal reward. This article offers a few gems from this priceless horde that awaits our investigation. This article also has as its intention the silencing of doubts about Scripture, Christ, and his gospel.

The most important day in the history of time and eternity was the day of Christ's crucifixion. It was a tragic day, unparalleled, but it was also miraculous and marvellous beyond measure. Never before had there been such cruelty, and never before had there been such love. It was a day that mirrored all of time. It symbolized and summarized all the outstanding events of the past, present and future. Those who come to understand this will never again be plagued by doubts regarding Scripture.

Have you ever read Habakkuk 3:4? Here it is: "His splendor was like the sunrise; rays flashed from his hand, where his power was hidden." Some translations use "side" rather than "hand," probably in the providence of God for when the Saviour comes again we will see glory streaming from his wounds. Forever the marks of Calvary will be honoured through eternal ages.

It all began in a manger long, long ago.

Have you ever considered the many ways in which Christ's birth prefigured his death at Golgotha? Here are some. We see him first as we behold him last—naked. His birth is at Bethlehem—the house of bread, and on the Cross that sacred Bread was broken for us. There was no room for the Christ child so he was born in a barn amid the sacrificial clean animals. At Calvary it was shown that we could find no room for God on this planet, so he was raised above it on the Cross—poised between heaven and earth. That Cross was an inverted sword with God's hand on the hilt caressing the rejected One.

A unique star in the heavens betokened the unique birth, and his death was accompanied by another heavenly sign—the midday midnight as stygian darkness covered the earth.

Wise men came from the East at his birth—the East symbolizes the past. But en route to Calvary we find a wise man from the West (Simon of Cyrene). The West symbolized the future. Past and future meet at the manger.

Myrrh was a gift to the Christ child and also to the dead Christ on his way to Joseph's new tomb. It was a compound of perfumes from other trees, and signified the saving aroma from the tree of Calvary. See Galatians 3:13; Acts 5:30; 10:39; 13:29; and 1 Peter 2:24.

The lovers and protectors of the newborn baby were Mary and Joseph, and at the Cross, we find Mary his mother and Joseph of Arimathea, who also loved the Savior. So Jesus came from a virgin womb and ended his earthly days in a virgin tomb that had never before been used.

Forty days after his birth we find him at the temple for dedication, and forty days after his resurrection He ascended to the heavenly temple for the dedication of the new covenant ministry. A Joseph protected the virgin womb, and another Joseph cared for the virgin tomb. Animals surrounded him in the manger, and Psalm 22 foretold that in his suffering he would be surrounded by "wild bulls" (the wicked).

The child was called Jesus, and the dying man fulfilled the name as he saved the fallen world ("He shall save their people from their sins"). Angels sang when he was born, and they greeted him on his rebirth—his resurrection. See Luke 2:9-14 and Matthew 28:2-7.

The newborn was wrapped in swaddling clothes, but the crucified Jesus was wrapped in fine linen and then glory. There were shepherds rejoicing at his birth, and there were shepherds (the disciples) sorrowing at his death though nowhere to be seen.

Four groups of people can be found at the birth and the dying. First there were those who sought truth like the Wise Men from the East, and like the penitent thief and the centurion thirty-three years later. In contrast there were also those who avoided the truth by worshipping their traditions and effete dogmas. They were the Jewish leaders with whom Herod counselled, and again we find them jeering at the Savior in his dying agonies.

A third group, similar to the second, wish to destroy the child and the man. They link with ignorant government officials and soldiers to do the work. A fourth group, including Mary and Joseph, are prepared to die to protect Jesus.

In both scenes Jesus is of course central for he is the mediator between God and men; he is the Daysman from on high. So we read concerning him that he was placed "in the midst" between the malefactors, and he remains "in the midst" in glory. See Revelation 1:13; 2:1; 2:7; 4:6; 5:6 and 7:17. Jesus is ever central, between the Father and the Spirit, between time and eternity, between law and grace, between us and condemnation and death.

To fall in love with the crucified Saviour is to find Paradise. So it was with the penitent thief. And so it is with every believer (see Luke 23:43).

It is vitally important that we recognize how Calvary rehearsed and undid the Fall in Eden. John 19:41, in order to remind us of Eden, tells us that there was a garden where Christ was crucified. Again we have two thieves, a naked Adam, a tree that is both the tree of life and the tree of knowledge of good and evil. Again, we have the serpent present and tempting. Satan through the Pharisees tempted Christ to save himself and come down from the cross. Also in Eden we have a sacrifice. See Genesis 3: 21, and the skins from that sacrifice hid the nakedness of the first sinners.

I beg of you to understand this. Many jeer at the story of Genesis chapter 3, the story of the great apostasy in Eden. It is considered by most to be a myth. But a close study of Calvary finds echoes of Eden and an undoing of that worst of all tragedies. The Fall was as much history as the Crucifixion. Moreover, the Fall was the cause of all that happened at Golgotha.

It was on the sixth day of the week that Adam, the head of the race, was put to sleep and had his side opened so that he might have a bride. So it was with the last Adam on Calvary. He also fell asleep in death on the sixth day of Passion Week, and his side was opened. The blood and the water that came from his side symbolized justification and sanctification which give birth to his bride—the church.

It should also be noted that in Genesis 2:17 the first Adam was warned that death would be the result of disobedience. So there was a death in Eden after the Fall as surely as there was a later death of the last Adam at Calvary. Spurgeon commented:

> That Adam did die in the day when he ate of the fruit is certain, or else the Lord spake not the truth. His nature was wrecked and ruined by separation from God and by a fall from that condition which constitutes the true life of man.
> The Treasury of the New Testament, Volume 3, page 44

According to 1 John 3:14, it is possible to be in a state of death though still existing. The last Adam also died as result of separation from God—"My God, my God, why hast thou forsaken me?" Thus did Calvary's events replay the history of the primeval past.

Even more than that, the day of the Cross not only points back to Eden but it points to today, to every day, every place, and every person on this planet. See Hebrews 6:6, which tells us that our sins crucify Christ afresh. We repeat Calvary each time we indulge self and count Christ of no value. Calvary is not just at Jerusalem. The place of the skull is not just at Golgotha. There is no place near you where Jesus is not being crucified. Every spot that is stained by sin, everywhere the commands of God are trampled upon, everywhere the Spirit is quenched and his restraint rejected—there is Calvary. It is even so in your heart, unless you have found the Redeemer.

Now, particularly, may I point out that the day of the Crucifixion has much to tell us about the last days of earth, about the end of the world. Hebrews 9:26 states that Christ died "at the end of the world." Legally, the world's judgment day was Calvary. There sin was atoned for, and transgressions and iniquity legally removed from the human race for all who would choose to accept the gift. See also 1 Corinthians 10:11.

The inscription on the Cross in three languages said that Christ was a king. Soon he was to be King of his church, the world and the universe. The thief referred to Christ's kingdom. And also to Paradise—the beautiful garden of Eden, which is to flourish again in the new world. See Revelation 2:7.

But more than that, the day of the Cross details to us the characteristic features of the "hour of trial that is going to come upon the whole world" (Revelation 3:10). I refer to what Christ called "the great tribulation" and the Old Testament "a time of trouble," even "a time of Jacob's trouble." See Matthew 24:21, Daniel 12:1 and Jeremiah 30:7. Everyone on the planet is to be tested just prior to Christ's Second Coming. See Revelation 3:10.

What we see at Calvary are the godless representatives of cruel government and apostate religion. They were united to "crush the wretch" (Voltaire's term). So it will be again with the body of Christ. The church is recurringly called his "body," and the body must go through the same experience as the head. The church, which is the body of Christ, is in one place even called Christ. See 1 Corinthians 12:12 and observe the last verses of Ephesians 1 and also Ephesians 4:15,16.

Many scholars have noted that Calvary was a microcosm of the end of the world. These include such well-known academics as Hendrikus Berkhof, R. H. Lightfoot, W. Grundmann, Alexander Maclaren and Austin Farrer. The latter, for example, states that "the substance of the last things and the substance of the Passion are one and the same" *(A Study in St. Mark,* page 285). A worldwide Calvary is coming when desperate and wicked powers will try with a cheap religion to beguile and control the whole world.

Passion Week beginning with the Triumphant Entry and closing with the death of Christ outlines in miniature all the main features of the last days of the body of Christ—his church. Have you ever noticed how Christ's sermons and his parables in this week chiefly revolve around the theme of judgment? They all point to Judgment Day.

Consider the cleansing of the temple, the cursing of the fig tree, the warning of destruction to the wicked husbandmen, the two sons, the wedding banquet and the death of the man without a wedding garment, the crushing stone, the removal of the kingdom from the Jewish race, the woes on the Pharisees (Matthew 23) and the Olivet Sermon, which speaks of the end of the Jewish world and the end of ours (Matthew 24 and 25, Mark 13, and Luke 21).

Consider the sequence: Christ enters triumphantly the capital city of Jerusalem, and people strew his pathway with palm branches and salute him as the Messiah about to establish his kingdom. This event polarizes the Jewish world, and in consequence the wicked apostate leaders plot Christ's death. Judas plans to betray his Lord; there is a time of agony in Gethsemane, followed by the greater time of trouble on the Cross.

So will it be in earth's last hours: the gospel will be proclaimed with power (Mark 13:10; Matt. 24:14: Rev. 18:1-4; Rev. 10:1-7; 11:3–12), and that will stir up the unbelieving world until a death decree is issued. See Revelation 13:11-18. The church will experience its Gethsemane and then its Calvary. Many will die. See Luke 21:12-17 and Daniel 12:7 and 11:36-44. However, for the Elect's sake, the days are shortened and signs in the sun, moon, and stars will announce the return of the glorious Son of God. See Matthew 24:29-31.

Berkhof summarized well:

In all synoptic Gospels statements about the future are summarized right before the Passion story. The themes dealt with are watchfulness, oppression, decrease of love, flight, and finally spectacular natural phenomena and the coming of the son of man in glory. It is conspicuous that all these themes recur in the following chapters which deal with Christ's suffering, death, and resurrection ... the meaning is obvious that the future will show—on a larger, and eventually world-wide scale—a repetition of what has happened in the crucifixion and resurrection of Christ. *Well-founded Hope*, pages 23–24

Key words of the Olivet sermon are "watch," "hour," and "betray." All these reoccur in the following chapters about Christ's last hours. Please understand this: Calvary was the first and chief Armageddon. Colossians 2:15 states that Christ fought and overcome principalities and powers at the Cross. Satan and his evil hosts were present, jeering and mocking, and tempting Christ to come down from the Cross.

Associated with this awful conflict came heavenly signs, darkness, then earthquake before resurrection with special mention of the Holy City. See Matthew 27:51-54. Read Revelation 16 about the final Armageddon when the hosts of Satan attempt to wipe out the church of Christ, but are themselves defeated by the return of the "kings of the east," Christ and his glorious armies from heaven. In that context also we find darkness, earthquake, wicked spirits and then the resurrections of Revelation 20 and the Holy City of chapters 21 and 22.

All of this was mirrored on that great and terrible day of the Crucifixion. It covered the past, the present, and the future. No human hand could have written the account. The typology, the echoes, and the forecasts are beyond human invention. This is the Hand of God. The Bible is true. The Son of God died for you and me. Paradise awaits us if we receive the word of Christ, if we believe his gospel. There is no other way.

Made in the USA
Charleston, SC
30 August 2015